Footpaths in fields of orange and yellow daisies, Biedouw Valley

Vygies, Naries Retreat

NAMAQUA SELF-DRIVE

Namaqualand, Nieuwoudtville & West Coast

Text & Photos by **Heléne Venter**

Published by
HPH Publishing

Gousblomme, pietsnot, vygies, Cape marigold, sambreeltjies, hongerblomme, gazanias and daisies, near Soebatsfontein

Yellow pietsnot (*Grielum humifusum*) and varkiesknolle (*Conicosia elongata*), Kamassies near Kamieskroon

Contents

NAMAQUALAND
NORTHERN CAPE
NIEUWOUDTVILLE
WEST COAST
WESTERN CAPE
Rosh Pinah
Ais-Ais
Karasburg
Ariamsvlei
Upington
Augrabies
Kakamas
Groblershoop
Oranjemund
Alexander Bay
Kuboes
Eksteenfontein
Vioolsdrif
Lekkersing
Pella
Pofadder
Aggeneys
Port Nolloth
McDougall's Bay
Steinkopf
Kenhardt
Concordia
Nababeep
Okiep
Springbok
Grootmis
Kleinzee
Nariés
Komaggas
Kamassies
Rooifontein
Bowesdorp
Soebatsfontein
Kamieskroon
Koingnaas
Hondeklipbaai
Leliefontein
Wallekraal
Karas
Klipfontein
Garies
Kliprand
Brandvlei
Rietpoort
Bitterfontein
Loeriesfontein
Nuwerus
Brand se Baai
Landplaas
Nieuwoudtville
Calvinia
Williston
Lutzville
Vanrhynsdorp
Vredendal
Klawer
Papendorp
Strandfontein
Doringbaai
Fraserburg
Lambert's Bay
Graafwater
Leipoldtville
Clanwilliam
Wupperthal
Eland's Bay
Sandberg
Redelinghuys
Sutherland
Klein Tafelberg
Citrusdal
Wamakersvlei
Dwarskersbos
St Helena Bay
Aurora
Paternoster
Velddrif
Port Owen
Tietiesbaai
Vredenburg
Piketberg
Jacobsbaai
Saldanha Bay
Koringberg
Langebaan
Hopefield
Porterville
Tulbagh
Yzerfontein
Darling
Riebeek Wes
Riebeek Kasteel
Ceres
Grotto Bay
Ganzekraal
Mamre
Malmesbury
Wellington
Paarl
Worcester
Oudtshoorn
Melkbosstrand
Montagu
Cape Town
Franschhoek
Stellenbosch
Swellendam
Gordan's Bay
Simon's Town
Grabouw
Caledon
Hermanus
Stanford
Still Bay
Gansbaai
Bredasdorp

Bittergousblom, orange daisies, surings, hongerblomme and vygies, Springbok golf course

Yellow knopieopslag (*Cotula* sp.), orange daisies, bittergousblom and white sporrie, between Port Nolloth and Steinkopf

DESOLATE ABUNDANCE

The contrasting notions of 'desolate' and 'abundance' create a tension that is rich in meaning and invites us to contemplate the idea that, even amid emptiness and loss, there can be hidden richness and beauty waiting to be discovered.

It is a concept that applies to many aspects of life; a landscape that is both barren and majestic, a person who is both lonely and resilient, or a moment that is both heartbreaking and inspiring.

Incredible abundance can sometimes be found in the most unexpected places. Renewal and growth are always possible. It is a reminder that life is complex and full of contradictions, and some meaningful experiences often lie at the intersection of opposing forces.

INTRODUCTION

The purpose of this book is to recount my more than 20-year expedition documenting the ever-changing landscapes of Namaqualand, Nieuwoudtville and the surrounding regions of the Hantam Karoo and West Coast in southern Africa.

What began as a simple project of photographing my hometown of Springbok soon expanded to include the diverse ecological treasures of the surrounding regions. These areas maintain a delicate balance between the environment's flora, fauna, climate and geology.

This book serves as a visual guide to these areas at their peak, helping readers plan their trips and choose the best routes and locations based on their available time.

These regions are barren and challenging for most of the year, with little to see during the dry seasons. However, a breathtaking transformation occurs when the winter nights shorten and the rains come. The once desolate landscape is blanketed in a magnificent array of rainbow-hued flowers, creating dazzling explosions of colour in the southern hemisphere.

The timing and duration of the flower season vary depending on rainfall, temperature and warm mountain winds. Typically, it commences at the end of July, peaks in August or September, and sometimes extends into October. However, this colourful display is ever-changing, with some flowers at their prime, others budding and some on the verge of fading away. Some years, clouds cover the country but no rain falls, resulting in little or no display of flowers, and no two consecutive years exhibit the same show.

The flowers captured in this book are not grown in artificial greenhouses. Instead, they have evolved to survive in harsh, marginal environments, multiplying before vanishing. It required many journeys to these distant locations to capture them at their zenith.

After the winter rains, these plants proliferate, blossom, produce seeds and perish within a few weeks. The short-lived exhibition soon vanishes in the scorching heat and wind, and the seeds fall back into the soil. They can remain dormant for years until suitable germination conditions arise.

Namaqualand's flora is one of the few global desert 'wasteland' biodiversity hotspots, meaning it is at significant risk of danger, harm or destruction.

Sambreeltjies (*Felicia* sp.), Naries Retreat

Bobbejaangesiggies (*Hemimeris* sp.), Namaqua National Park

A white horse and white rain daisies, Nieuwoudtville

How to plan your wildflower experience

Spring in the flower-rich regions of Namaqualand, Nieuwoudtville, Cederberg and the West Coast is a captivating but capricious spectacle and typically unfolds from August to late September. However, even with average winter rainfall, accurately predicting the exact intensity and timing of the spring bloom can be challenging. Reliable forecasts often materialise only around July, and the precise blooming period is not clear until it's underway – unfortunately, often too late for convenient accommodation bookings.

Deep red vygies, Waylands (Darling)

Oxblood, Boereplaas

Where are the best places to see the wildflowers and when is the best time?

- **Nieuwoudtville:** Blooms typically appear from late July to late August, often with a more extended season lasting up to six weeks.
- **Namaqualand:** Mid to late August offers the best viewing opportunities. However, in the Kamiesberg, the blooming period may start only in September.
- **Clanwilliam and the Cederberg:** Peak bloom is expected from mid to late August.
- **West Coast:** The optimal window for flower viewing is typically late August to late September, sometimes extending into October.

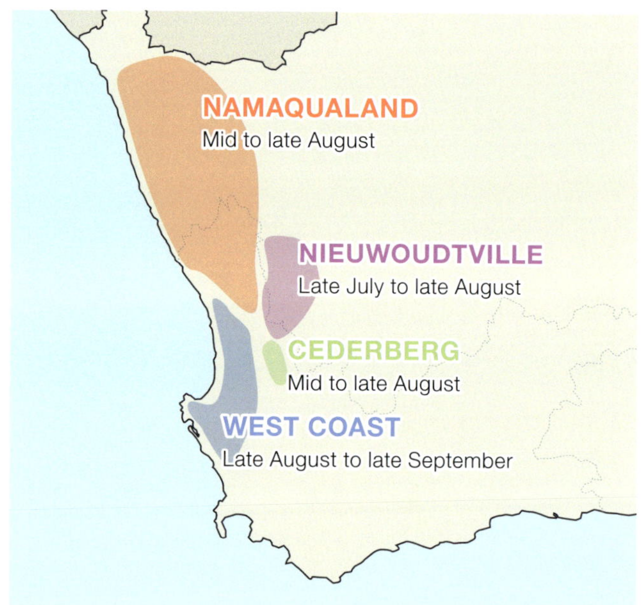

Sterretjie (*Pauridia serrata*), Paternoster

Knopiesopslag (*Lasiospermum brachyglossum*)

Bittergousblom

How long to go for?

A comprehensive tour encompassing all these regions will likely maximise your chances of encountering the floral displays at all blooming stages, as some areas may be at their peak, others just beginning to bloom, and some may have already passed their prime. However, not all of us have the luxury of so much time on hand.

- Decide **how much time you have** and what area you want to visit, then aim for the best dates for that area over that time. The end of August is perhaps a safe starting point for your trip.
- **Begin your journey at Nieuwoudtville**, move then to the more **northerly** flower regions, like Namaqua National Park and Springbok. Warmer temperatures result in earlier blooms, as not all flowers bloom simultaneously. Later-blooming species and bulbs ensure an extended flower season.
- Gradually **move southwards**, exploring regions like the Biedouw Valley, West Coast National Park and Darling as the bloom progresses.

Scented candelabra lily or Maartblom (*Brunsvigia bosmaniae*), Hantam National Botanical Garden, Nieuwoudtville

Pienkkwas (*Haemanthus amarylloides*), Boereplaas, Nieuwoudtville

Getting there

- The best way to explore Namaqualand is by car for maximum flexibility.
- You can experience the wildflowers through self-drives, walking trails or bicycle routes.
- Explore scenic backroads to discover hidden floral treasures and the freedom to stop and immerse yourself in the flowers.
- If you would prefer a more comprehensive and immersive experience, private guided tours can take you through different fields, farmlands and wild valleys.
- Day trips are ideal for those with limited time. Whether you're in Cape Town and want to explore the blooming wildflowers of the southern West Coast (late August/early September) or are already in the flower region and looking for scenic routes, a private or self-guided day tour is a great way to experience the beauty of the area.

White sporrie (*Heliophila* sp.), Namaqua National Park

White flax, Boereplaas, Nieuwoudtville

White vygies (*Monilaria obconica Aizoaceae*) with bright yellow centres, Naries Retreat

Tips for optimal flower viewing

- Check the weather when planning your trips: Flowers will not open if it's too cold or cloudy. Overcast skies and rain significantly diminish the flower display. Plan alternative activities for such days
- The best time to see the flowers is in full daylight, when the sun is at its highest, between 10:30 and 15:30, and they have fully opened. The perfect temperature for viewing wildflowers is around 14°C.
- Plan your daily route with the sun at your back to enhance the viewing experience.
- If you can, try to visit the wildflower locations during the week when there are fewer visitors.
- Take note of gate opening times at parks and reserves and get there before they open.
- Step out of your car, where you safely and properly can do so, and immerse yourself in the beauty of the flowers. You will gain a much deeper appreciation.
- Please refrain from picking the flowers and lying in them. Do not drive on the flowers. Some parks restrict visitors from walking in them.
- A printed flower map can serve as a simple flower guide. Such maps are readily available at local tourism offices or most guesthouses. They often provide photos and names of common blooms, enriching your understanding.

Phone the flower hotline or local tourism office for the most up-to-date information on areas with the best flower displays. They can help you with last-minute accommodation enquiries, as they generally know who has the last room to sell.

When you are on your way, visit Flowers of Namaqualand and the West Coast Facebook page, or email Weskus Tourism to be added to their Flower Update mailing list (tourism@wcdm.co.za). They send out a weekly update on where the best flowers are in the various areas of the Western Cape. (NB. This does not include Nieuwoudtville or areas further north of Vredendal.)

Namaqua National Park

Dense clusters of pietsnot (*Grielum humifusum*), Kamassies, Kamiesberg

Thousands of Cape marigolds (*Arctotheca calendula*), Darling

Tourist information and telephone numbers

Phone the flower hotline or local tourism office for the most up-to-date information on areas with the best flower displays.

- West Coast Flower Line – 063 639 3532 for regular updates on spring flowers, flower shows and weather forecasts during the flower season
- Weskus Flowers – tourism@wcdm.co.za
- Paternoster – 074 283 5474
- Cape Columbine Nature Reserve – 022 752 2718
- St Helena Bay – 074 283 5474
- West Coast National Park, Postberg Nature Reserve is open only in August and September – 022 772 2144
- Darling Wildflower Show is usually held over the third weekend of September – 068 151 5692 darlingwildflowers.co.za
- Hopefield Annual Fynbos Show. Held over the last weekend of August – 063 406 0421 hopefieldfynbos.co.za
- Darling Wildflower Society – 068 151 5692
- Darling Tourism – 022 492 3361
- Waylands Wildflower Reserve – 022 492 2873
- Contreberg – 072 717 1607
- Clanwilliam Tourism Office – 027 482 2024
- Clanwilliam Flower Show – www.clanflora.co.za
- Vanrhynsdorp Tourism Office – 027 201 3376
- Nieuwoudtville (ask for a map and guidance for the best flowers) – 027 218 1336
- Namaqualand – 072 760 6019
- Pilansii Tours – 082 492 8291
- Garies Tourist Stall (ask for a map and guidance for the best flowers) – 027 652 1220
- Goegap Nature Reserve – 027 718 9906
- Kamieskroon Hotel and Information Centre – 027 983 2831
- Namaqua National Park at Kamieskroon – 027 672 1948
- Springbok – 053 832 2657/027 712 8036

Cape marigold (*Arctotheca calendula*), Darling

Flower ratings

The flower ratings offer an average indication, reflecting observations over the 20 years this book covers. However, actual blooming can change significantly based on rainfall, temperature, wind and other ever-changing weather conditions.

It's important to remember, even areas that rarely bloom can unexpectedly burst into a startling profusion of colour with good rain and favourable weather conditions.

Before you travel, contact the tourist information or flower hotline for the latest flower updates. You will find a list of phone numbers for each area on page 31.

White rain daisies and blue sporrie, Verlorenvlei

Town name

Best time to visit for flower displays

Wildflowers commonly seen in this area

Highlights

General information about the town. The tab on the top left of the page shows the rough position of the town. The colour of the tab indicates the region (Namaqualand orange, Nieuwoudtville pink and West Coast blue).

* little flower displays, not annual

** occasional flower displays, not annual

*** moderate flower displays appearing after rainfall

**** abundant flower displays after significant rainfall

***** spectacular flower displays after substantial rainfall

Mauve manulea, Garies

Blue sporrie (*Heliophila coronopifolia*), Verlorenvlei

Remarkable adaptations of plants to ensure survival in arid regions

Colour

Colour plays a crucial role in attracting pollinators, which are essential for pollen dispersal. Flowers offer attractive incentives to entice these visitors to ensure the continuation of their species.

Petals

Petals are modified leaves that encircle a flower's reproductive parts. They serve two primary functions: protection and attraction. Petals attract specific pollinators, such as bees, butterflies and birds, by displaying various colours, patterns and shapes. These visual cues can also guide pollinators towards the flower's nectar or pollen, ensuring successful pollination.

Scent

Flowers can emit scents to attract desirable pollinators or repel undesirable ones. Some even mimic the smell of decaying matter to lure specific insects.

Nyctinasty

Nyctinasty is the circadian rhythm-based nastic movement of higher plants in response to the onset of darkness, or a plant 'sleeping'.

Most of Namaqualand's springtime blooms belong to the *Asteraceae*, one of Earth's most prominent flowering families. Often called 'day's eye', they exhibit nyctinasty, closing their petals at night and reopening at dawn.

Succulents

With their fleshy, swollen leaves, stems or roots, succulents are uniquely adapted to survive in arid environments. Often sporting spines or tiny, rarely bright green leaves, their unusual appearance is a testament to their remarkable ability to withstand the harsh conditions of the desert.

Geophytes

Geophytes are perennial plants that survive adverse seasons (like drought or cold) by storing energy in underground organs such as bulbs, tubers, corms or rhizomes. These storage organs allow the plant to remain dormant when conditions are harsh and then quickly sprout leaves and flowers when favourable conditions – like rain in spring – return. Geophytes are especially common in Mediterranean-type climates like Namaqualand, where they take advantage of short, wet growing seasons.

Drought avoidance

Annual plants escape unfavourable conditions by not existing. They mature in a single season, then die, after channelling all their life energy into producing seeds for continued survival, leaving no plant material behind in the dry times.

Namaqua National Park (*Zaluzianskya collina*)

Namaqualand

NAMAQUALAND

The cultural heritage of Namaqualand dates back to ancient times, spanning hundreds of thousands of years. Archaeological discoveries include hand axes believed to have been crafted by Homo erectus, indicating this earliest known human presence could have lived in the area. More recently, the San people – a hunter-gatherer society – resided in the region and adapted their movements according to the availability of game, edible plants and water sources.

Namaqua ('Nama-kwa') means Nama Khoi people's land. The written history of Namaqualand dates back to the late 17th century when European explorers arrived in the region to investigate copper deposits among the Namaqua people in the north. After several unsuccessful expeditions, Simon van der Stel, the Governor of the Cape Colony, led a successful expedition in 1685 and returned with samples of copper ore and a collection of coloured drawings illustrating the flora and fauna they encountered during their journey.

Namaqualand is a region that spans Namibia and South Africa. The area's terrain varies from a rugged and arid landscape in the west to semi-desert in the northeast. Despite its harsh conditions, Namaqualand is known for its rich cultural history, abundant minerals, beauty and unique features, such as its wildflowers during spring.

A thriving copper and diamond mining industry has given rise to small towns near mission stations or water points throughout the region. The barren and desolate landscape, characterised by droughts, heat mirages and dust clouds, is imbued with an anticipation and longing for rain that never wanes. The rainfall in Namaqualand is mostly below 250 mm and can be as low as 50 mm per year. Water scarcity poses a significant challenge for human and livestock consumption, exacerbated by the limited effectiveness of storage dams owing to evaporation. Water supplies are largely obtained from springs and boreholes. The Orange River is the primary water source for the region, and the vegetation is sparse and stunted.

Despite its harsh conditions, the area is transformed by the arrival of rain and soon the once-barren earth is transformed into a life-boasting flowering garden creating a brief, yet stunning, display in early spring, showcasing a luxuriant array of colours that are unmatched in their breathtaking beauty anywhere else in the world. The fragrances of wildflowers intoxicate the senses, and the exquisite range of unique flora coexisting within just a few metres of each other is truly a sight to behold. Its beauty and resilience never cease to amaze and inspire.

Fields of Namaqualand daisies (*Dimorphotheca sinuata*), Kamiesberg near Kamieskroon

A typical daisy of the *Senecio* genus

Quick facts about Namaqualand

Namaqualand is a region in southern Africa renowned for its stunning spring wildflower displays and unique desert landscapes. The area spans parts of both South Africa and Namibia, divided by the Orange River into two sections: **Little Namaqualand** is in South Africa's Northern Cape province, and **Great Namaqualand** lies in southern Namibia. This book deals only with Little Namaqualand, but the Richtersveld is not included.

Why the area is great for succulent Karoo vegetation

Geology, topography, soils and climate determine the biodiversity of an area.

- Some of the **oldest rocks on Earth** underlie the Namaqua area, showing signs of intense folding and faulting from ancient mountain-building events.
- **Low mountain ranges**, **hills** and **inselbergs** (isolated rocky hills rising from plains) shape the landscape. The **Kamiesberge** is an ancient, weathered granite mountain range in the area.
- Much of the terrain consists of **arid plateaus** with stony, sandy soils, punctuated by ephemeral rivers and **dry riverbeds** (called ***riviere***).
- The soils of Namaqualand are shallow, often derived directly from the weathering of underlying rocks. They support **Succulent Karoo vegetation**, adapted to drought and nutrient-poor conditions.
- Towards the Atlantic Ocean, the land flattens into a narrow **coastal plain**, including parts of the **Namaqua National Park**.
- To the north, the **Orange River** marks the boundary between Little and Great Namaqualand. The **Olifants River** from east to west is the southern marker for Namaqualand's southern boundary.

Top places to explore

- **Namaqua National Park (Skilpad)**, **Soebatsfontein** and **Spoegrivier**: Located west of the N7, this park is famed for its vibrant spring wildflower blooms and diverse succulent flora. These are part of the Caracal Eco Route.
- **Springbok**, **Goegab Nature Reserve, Groothoog near Concordia** and **Nababeep**: Situated near Springbok, this section offers scenic landscapes and various plant species.
- **Garies**: Situated on the N7.

Biodiversity

The unique geology and topography give rise to the **Succulent Karoo biome**, a biodiversity hotspot with over **3500 plant species**, with as much as 40% of them being endemic (this means they are found nowhere else on Earth). It is especially famous for the **spring wildflower displays**, which bloom after winter rains. Plant types of Namaqualand exhibit special adaptations that help them to survive in this harsh, arid environment.

Botanical richness

- **Succulents** have thick fleshy leaves or stems for water storage. They also have minimal surfaces to reduce water loss, most of which can grow in rock crevices or sandy soils. Succulents are the dominant group overall.
- **Geophytes** are prolific during the spring bloom (August–October); their underground bulbs and tubers store water to survive drought. Explosive flowering after rain quickly attracts pollinators.
- **Low shrubs** and **dwarf shrublands** grow on rocky slopes, gravel plains and dry valleys.
- **Annual herbs** and **wildflowers** are short-lived but spectacular in springtime. They germinate swiftly after winter rains and flower for a few weeks in spring.
- **Lichens** and **mosses** are found in rocky and coastal areas and thrive in fog zones and shaded crevices. They are crucial in microhabitats and soil crust formations.

Animal biodiversity

Many animals in Namaqualand are **active only at night** to avoid the extreme heat.

Water efficiency is essential; therefore, some animals never drink water directly, getting moisture from food. The key to survival for others is to use **camouflage** to blend into the rocky and sandy landscape.

- **Pollinators** are essential during the flowering time; therefore, expect to find a large selection of beetles, butterflies, flies, solitary bees and sunbirds.
- **Amphibians** are rare but around and squeaky rain frogs emerge after rains to mate.
- **Reptiles** abound and, if you are lucky, you may encounter a Namaqua chameleon or a padloper tortoise (rare) and find lots of geckos and skinks at night.
- Most **mammals** are nocturnal, small and stealthy. You may encounter caracal, bat-eared and Cape foxes, aardvarks, aardwolf, klipspringer and many small rodents such as gerbils, mice and mole rats.
- **Birds** commonly seen include buntings, chats, canaries, Namaqua sandgrouse, black harrier (rare), Cape sparrows, bokmakierie and sunbirds.

Metre-high skaapbos (*Tripteris oppsitifolia*), near Naries Retreat

Yellow knopiesopslag, purple vygies, white sporrie, pink hongerblomme, orange daisies and gousblomme, near Soebatsfontein Gate, Namaqua National Park

Springbok

Late August

Daisies, gousblom, pietsnot, Cape marigold, surings, vygies, various succulents

Goegap Nature Reserve, Springbok Cultural Hoogte, Blue Mine, hiking, Namaqua museum, stargazing

Springbok is situated in a narrow valley enclosed by the Klein Koperberge's towering, multi-coloured rocks, with a small hillock at its centre. The town's origins can be traced back to the farm Melkboschkuil, owned by Kowie Cloete. It was initially known as Springbokfontein, owing to the abundance of antelope in the area (a translation of the Khoikhoi word 'guchas' means 'springbok'). In 1862, this location was designated as a copper mining core and the name Springbokfontein was eventually shortened to Springbok in 1911.

According to John M Smalberger, in *A History of Copper Mining in Namaqualand*, mining began at Springbokfontein after being purchased from Mr Langkowie Cloete on behalf of the company Phillips and King in 1850. The first mining began almost immediately. Smalberger tells us the farm was bought on 16 March 1850. In 1862, Phillips and King was bought by John Taylor and Sons, London, and became the Cape Copper Mining Company, later to be called the Cape Copper Company.

The town developed into an administration centre for copper mining operations in the region, and even though the mining activities declined, Springbok remained an important regional capital. Today, the town relies on tourism, commerce and farming for its livelihood. And mining is reviving in the surrounding areas.

Highway to Springbok

Orange Namaqualand daisies (*Dimorphotheca sinuata*)

Orange daisies, gousblom, hongerblomme and vygies, Springbok golf course

Purple and yellow hongerblomme, orange daisies, beetle daisies, pietsnot and yellow gansogies, Silwerfontein farm near Springbok

Orange daisies and a dash of pietsnot, Silwerfontein farm near Springbok

Orange daisies and pietsnot, Silwerfontein farm near Springbok

Goegap

Goegap Nature Reserve

✳✳✳✳✳

- Mid to end August; in a good year, spectacular wildflower displays
- Daisies, gousblom, vygies, various succulents, kapokbos, sporries
- Hiking trails, mountain biking, birding, accommodation, 4x4 trails, desert-adapted plants: Hester Malan Nature Reserve

The Nature Reserve at Goegap (meaning 'waterhole') was originally known as Hester Malan Nature Reserve. It was started with a generous donation of agricultural land by the O'Okiep Copper Company. This land, initially used as grazing grounds for livestock, was repurposed in 1966 to create a flower reserve. The reserve was further developed in 1969 when it was fenced, and various wildlife species were introduced.

Later, the reserve expanded with the acquisition of the Goegap farm by Cape Nature and Environmental Directorate. Today, this breathtaking reserve, meandering amid rugged granite peaks and sandy plains, hosts almost 600 indigenous flower species.

One of the reserve's original objectives was to create a flower garden. Within Goegap Nature Reserve is the Hester Malan Wild Flower Garden, named after the cherished wife of Nico Malan, who at the time served as administrator of the Cape of Good Hope. This haven showcases a stunning array of succulents indigenous to the region, some boasting such rarity they exist nowhere else on Earth.

Bittergousblom, hongerblomme and vygies, Goegap Nature Reserve.

White knopiesopslag (*Cotula laxa, Asteraceae*), Goegap Nature Reserve

Vygies, daisies, hongerblomme, knopiesopslag and gousblom, Goegap Nature Reserve

Gousblom, orange daisies, yellow and purple hongerblomme, sambreeltjies and vygies, Goegap Nature Reserve

Orange daisies, yellow hongerblomme, Cape marigold (*Arctotheca calendula*), Okiep

Okiep

- **Mid to end August; in a good year, many beautiful flowers all over town**
- **Daisies, gousblom, Cape marigold, vygies, surings**
- **Copper mining history, mine tours (historical), Anglican church, Namaqua War Memorial**

Although evidence suggests the Namaqua people may have been mining copper for several centuries before the arrival of European settlers in Africa, the first discovery by these settlers of the copper deposits in this area was made by Simon van der Stel's expedition in 1685, near what in the late 20th century became the Carolusberg mine. The Namaqualand region in the Northern Cape Province encompasses the O'Okiep copper district, spanning an estimated area of around 3 000 square kilometres. Within this district, you will find the towns of Springbok, Nababeep, Okiep, Concordia and Carolusberg. The district became the location of the first mines opened by Europeans in South Africa. The first South African mining company can probably be said to be the South African Mining Company, which was founded in 1846. However, the mine achieved very little, and faded from existence shortly after 1848. One of its directors was John King, of Phillips and King, which became the first company to start mining after the purchase of Springbokfontein in 1850.

Springbok is known as the oldest mining town in South Africa. Mining began at O'Okiep in 1856. The original prospect was a single outcrop, 6 m across. The O'Okiep mine quickly surpassed the Springbokfontein mine in importance, and went on to become the richest copper mine in the world.

The town's name is derived from the Nama word U-gieb, which translates as 'the large brackish place'.

The spelling of the name changed to Okiep in the 1970s; the O'Okiep Copper Company, however, retained the original spelling. This town was once the central hub of activity within the O'Okiep copper district owing to the richness of its copper deposits. However, the First World War caused problems in the industry, and the once-mighty Cape Copper Company shut down overnight in April 1919. When copper mining in the area restarted significantly, with the inception of the O'Okiep Copper Company in 1937, the operation's headquarters were at Nababeep. All the towns of the Copper District were involved in the resurge of activity, which lasted until the closure of the O'Okiep Copper Company in 2004.

Okiep still bears witness to the history of its early mining days, with abandoned mining equipment, including remnants imported from Cornwall, scattered about, now a bittersweet reminder of its once-bustling past.

The wind sways the orange daisies, gousblomme, yellow hongerblomme and Cape marigolds, Okiep

Dam and windpump set among bittergousblom, orange daisies, gansogies and pietsnot, Groothoog, near Concordia

Concordia

- **Mid to end August; good flower spot at Groothoog before Concordia, many spectacular flower displays**
- **Namaqualand daisies, gousblom, Cape marigold, pietsnot, vygies, sporries**
- **Copper mining village, copper mining history, old ore chutes, mine museum, old church, local culture exploration, photography**

Concordia, established initially as a Rhenish mission station in 1852, witnessed the onset of copper mining in the subsequent year, with the founding of the Namaqua Mining Company (later the Namaqua Copper Company) by Albert von Schlicht, who had first tried, unsuccessfully, to buy the farm at Springbokfontein. The Namaqua Copper Company remained in operation until 1983. Concordia served as the Boers' headquarters during the siege of O'Okiep in 1902.

The town's foundation is deeply intertwined with its mining heritage. Even before colonial times, the local indigenous people, the Khoisan or the Nama, extracted raw copper from the area. They skilfully fashioned this copper into alluring decorative pieces like neck adornments and bangles. As Dutch settlers arrived in the region, they were also drawn to the area's copper riches, embarking on numerous expeditions into the prosperous copper mountains. The exquisite decorative metal items were used to create and show off the settlers' wealth and status.

Bittergousblom (*Arctotis fastuosa*), near Concordia

Bittergousblom, orange daisies, white sporrie and pietsnot, Groothoog, near Concordia

Rusted car surrounded by daisies, gousblomme and pietsnot, Jakkalswater

Nababeep

- Late August to September; perfect flower spot
- Namaqualand daisies, mainly Ursinia, but look for others, gousblom, gazania, vygies
- Copper mine (viewpoints), 'Clara' mountain engine, smelter tours (check availability), historical buildings, panoramic views

Once known as Lelykepad, which translates to 'ugly road' in Afrikaans, the farm underwent a name change and became Nababeep, meaning 'rhinoceros place'. It is said the new name finds its roots in the Nama language and translates as Naba, signifying the 'hump of an animal', while 'beep' refers to a small spring.

In the 1850s, mining operations commenced, slowly at first, but eventually propelling Nababeep into becoming a prominent centre for copper extraction. A railway line linked Port Nolloth to O'Okiep, Concordia and Nababeep.

From 1876, ore was taken to Port Nolloth by train for export. In 1919, the mines of the Cape Copper Company faced closure as a result of a decline in the copper market. It was not until 1937, with the founding of the O'Okiep Copper Company, that the Nababeep mine reopened, and Nababeep became the headquarters of the company.

A remarkable vestige from the mining era is Clara, a narrow-gauge steam locomotive that was instrumental in transporting copper ore to Port Nolloth. A large part of Clara's exhibit has been moved from the Mining Museum at Nababeep to the Okiep Hotel and now holds a place of honour as a permanent display. During the flower season, the abandoned mining slopes are transformed into a breathtaking spectacle of deep orange daisies blossoming amid colossal boulders, enhancing the town's natural charm.

Deep orange daisies (berggousblom – *Ursinia calenduliflora*) thrive in the crevices of the granite koppies, Nababeep

Orange daisies (berggousblom – *Ursinia calenduliflora*) flourish between stoic granite koppies, Nababeep

Namaqualand daisy (*Ursinia cakilefolia*), Nababeep

Nababeep's landscape is claimed by deep orange daisies

Steinkopf

- Mid to end August; good flower displays in a good year
- Namaqualand daisies, gousblom, vygies, sporries
- Nama culture, historical mission station, Namaqua landscapes, flower viewing (seasonal), historical sites, Kindle Monument, Klipfontein graves, Anenous station and Nonahams, Rhenish Mission Church, Old Klipfontein railway station, Kookfontein eye, Immanuel Succulent Nursery, hiking tours

Brave and adventurous missionaries ventured into the unknown to spread their faith and convert the Nama to Christianity. The Nama practised polygamy and ancestor worship, presenting the missionaries with many challenges. They had to navigate unfamiliar terrain to find food, water and shelter. However, their dedication to the cause was unwavering, a quality that commands admiration. As a testament to their efforts, numerous towns in the area sprung up around churches or gathering places, as documented by historical records.

The history of Steinkopf begins with the Nama people. They settled at a spring a few kilometres south of where the town stands today. This spot was originally called Tarrakois or Bezondermijd, which means 'peculiar girl'.

In 1818, Reverend Heinrich Schmelen of the London Missionary Society arrived and established a mission station. He named it Steinkopf in honour of Dr Karl Steinkopf, a benefactor who generously donated to the mission's development.

The Nama community gradually moved north to an area with a permanent spring called Goegaas. The mission station followed in 1821, and the settlement became known as Kookfontein, which means 'boiling spring' in Afrikaans.

The Rhenish Mission Society took over the station in 1840. Reverend Ferdinand Brecher built a new church and school and changed the name back to Steinkopf.

Nowadays, Steinkopf is a hub for communal stock farming.

White sporrie, near Steinkopf

The unsually desolate landscape shines with yellow flowers, between Port Nolloth and Steinkopf

Port Nolloth

* - *****

- **Mid to end August; very little or no flowers around town, but beautiful between Steinkopf and Port Nolloth in an excellent year with spectacular flower displays**
- **Daisies, gousblom, vygies, succulents**
- **Coastal town, fishing, beach walks, diamond history museum, lighthouse, gateway to the Richtersveld region, known for its 4x4 trails and wildflowers, beach; holiday destination at McDougall's Bay**

Early town records describe the enormously harsh conditions experienced by those courageous enough to live there. It has meagre rainfall and a reliance on fog, which is eagerly obtained and harvested by plant life and small creatures that rely on it for survival.

Port Nolloth was originally known as Auquatowa in Nama and later as Robbebaai (bay of seals), since the Nama obtained a source of income from selling seal skins and dried seal meat.

To find a suitable sheltered harbour for copper ore shipments from the nearby O'Okiep and Springbok mines, Captain MS Nolloth founded Port Nolloth in 1855. Little happened there until 1869, when a railway was built from Port Nolloth to the mines and a town gradually developed. However, copper mining declined in the early 20th century, as did the shipments.

Fortune changed again in 1926 when alluvial diamonds were discovered on the coast, deposited with the aid of the Orange River, attracting a new wave of fortune seekers to the area. Despite the challenging task of finding precious stones, skilled divers still trawl the chilly seas for treasure.

From ore and gemstones to fish, this town has emerged from the desert to become the only tourist-friendly town along the Diamond coast, as access to other settlements was prohibited by mining companies that owned them. Nowadays, some fishing and tourism are the primary activities in Port Nolloth.

Daisies (*Othonna* sp.), Port Nolloth

Naries Retreat

✱✱ - ✱✱✱✱✱

- Mid to end August; medium to excellent in a good year
- Namaqualand daisies, gousblom, vygies, Pelargonium, succulents
- Luxury accommodation, scenic landscapes, hiking, stargazing, Namaqualand experience, cycling, hiking

Naries is a charming and romantic hideaway on the edge of the Spektakelberg between Springbok and Kleinzee.

The word Naries comes from the Nama language, meaning 'place where reeds grow', although the exact location of these reeds is uncertain. The area's isolation offers nature's soothing sounds, clean air and delicious food, making it an ideal oasis for rejuvenating your soul.

Years of overgrazing and unsustainable farming techniques in the past had damaged the land and vegetation of Naries. To restore it, all commercial goat farming ceased, and various native plant species were reintroduced.

Yellow blooms unite to form a picture-perfect garden, Naries Retreat.

Surings, Naries Retreat

Koingnaas

Kommagas

Mid to end August

Namaqualand daisies, gousblom, vygies

Cycling, Namaqua culture, scenic drives, flower viewing

This town is situated on the Kommagas River, a branch of the Buffels River.

The London Missionary Society established it as a mission station in 1829. Subsequently, the Rhenish Missionary Society took over and, eventually, the Dutch Reformed Church took charge in 1936. The name means 'place of many wild olive trees'.

Nature's magic in full display

White sporrie

Vygies, Kleinzee

Olifantsoutslaai (*Mesembryanthemum barklyi*)

Kleinzee

- **Late August; very little or no flowers around town**
- **Namaqualand daisies, vygies, dune fynbos species**
- **Diamond mining history, beach access (restricted in some areas), birding, coastal scenery, shipwreck 4x4 trails, Kleinzee museum, diamond mining tours, Kleinzee Nature Reserve, seals at the coast, cycling**

In 1927, diamonds were discovered at Kleyne Zee, a lagoon where the Buffels River meets the ocean. This discovery quickly led to the opening of a crater. Interestingly, despite the typically dry nature of the riverbed, a substantial underground water table near the surface made the location ideal for a small diamond-mining town.

The Cape Coast Exploration Company purchased the area in 1927 and it became part of De Beers the following year under the Namaqualand Mines Division of De Beers. Kleinzee was established in 1942 as a private settlement for alluvial diamond mining. The mining company exercised dominance over the entire region for an extended period. During this time, the area remained off-limits to visitors as diamond extraction operations consumed its resources.

By the 2000s, the diamond reserves had been depleted. Consequently, the property was sold and the town was transferred to the local municipality. Access-control measures were lifted and an environmental recovery programme was initiated.

Today, Kleinzee stands as a tranquil civilian village. The absence of mining activities has given the town a unique charm and serenity. The area is blessed with untouched coastal zones, indigenous vegetation further inland, dry semi-desert landscapes and the picturesque shoreline of the Atlantic Ocean on its western side.

Koingnaas

Mid to end August; few flowers around town, but beautiful displays towards Soebatsfontein

Daisies, gousblom, vygies, sporries

Remote Namaqualand experience, scenic beauty, stargazing, photography, shipwreck 4x4 trails

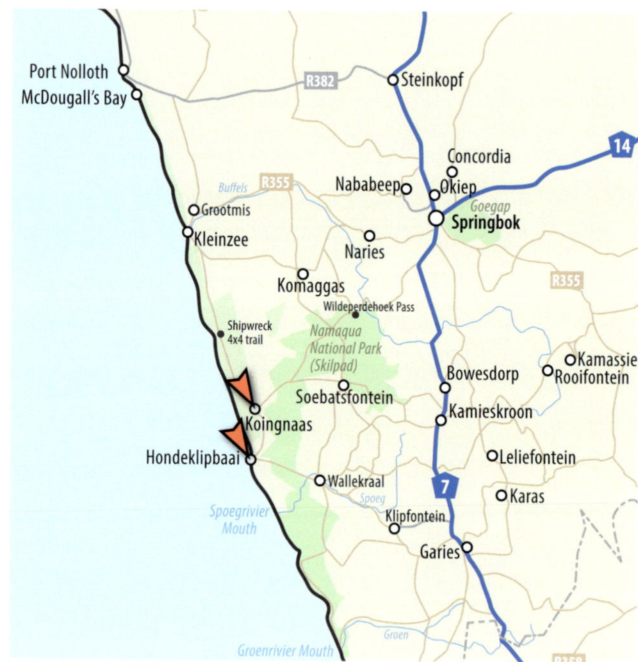

In 1970, De Beers Mining Company built the once-thriving little town along the Swartlintjies River to support its diamond mining operations. When production at the De Beers mines ceased in 2010, the population fell rapidly, and the local municipality took over the privately owned settlement in 2016.

Koingnaas derives its name from the Nama language, referring to a salty or salt spring. The original farm may have been named after the salty seawater that welled up during spring tides. However, both Koingnaas and Hondeklipbaai are supplied with fresh water from a water fountain located about 3.5 km north of Koingnaas, fitted with six borehole pumps.

Blue sporrie and white rain daisies (*Dimorphotheca pluvialis*), near Koingnaas

Yellow gazanias paint the coastline, near *Aristea* shipwreck

Hondeklipbaai

- Late August; there are very few or no flower displays around town, but there are beautiful displays past the *Aristea* shipwreck in a good year
- Daisies, vygies, dune fynbos species, Pelargonium
- Coastal walks, fishing, crayfishing (seasonal, permits needed), remote beach experience, lighthouse, *Aristea* shipwreck, Caracal Eco Route, beach, cycling, shipwreck 4x4 trail, fishing opportunities

In 1846, an intrepid adventurer, sea captain and trader, Thomas Grace, discovered a small natural bay on the Namaqualand coast. Hondeklipbaai earned its name from a rock formation resembling a seated dog near what became the police station in the village that was built there.

Initially, the village was a vital port for exporting copper to the United Kingdom. The Bosphorus vessel began to ship copper to Wales in 1852, with ore transported by ox wagons from the nearby mining towns of Springbok, Okiep and Nababeep. However, the treacherous seas and dense fog along the West Coast posed significant hazards, causing damage or shipwrecks to many vessels carrying the precious cargo. As a result, in the late 1860s, a safer harbour was established in Port Nolloth, superseding the original pier in the village.

The village's growth has been limited owing to its semi-desert surroundings and scarce water resources. It has gradually transformed into a tranquil fishing community, where the primary catch is rock lobster. The ebb and flow of the tides dictate the villagers' daily lives, while Hondeklipbaai remains a serene haven, offering respite from the bustling pace of city life.

Aristea shipwreck, Hondeklipbaai

Soebatsfontein

- **Late August; sometimes little or no flowers, but spectacular displays in a good year**
- **Namaqualand daisies, beetle daisies, gousblom, gazania, vygies, sporries**
- **Scenic drives, wildflower hotspot (seasonal, in good year), quaint village, Namaqua landscapes, photography, walking trails, accommodation, close to entrance of Namaqua National Park's entrance gate, 4x4 trails, cycling**

Nestled at the base of the escarpment, this charming village derives its name from the central spring, known as the 'begging' or 'pleading fountain'. According to local legend, in 1798, a man named Hendrik Stievert met a tragic fate at the hands of a group of San (Bushmen) despite pleading for his life.

Founded in the early 1900s, the town began as a cattle and animal farming centre and later transitioned to producing wool, mohair and karakul pelts. The town boasts a rich cultural tapestry. Many residents trace their ancestry back to the indigenous Khoi and San who have called this land home for millennia.

Visitors flock to explore the welcoming, contrasting surroundings of Namaqua National Park renowned for its breathtaking landscapes and vibrant wildflowers.

Slopes of colourful flowers near Soebatsfontein

Yellow ossierapuis (*Othonna cylindrica*) among white rain daisies and orange gousblomme, near Soebatsfontein

White sporrie, mauve vygies, yellow knopiesopslag, gazanias, perdebos and surings, near Soebatsfontein

Fields of vibrant flowers among granite koppies, close to Soebatsfontein

Wildeperdehoek Pass

- Mid August to beginning September; scenic views, a variety of individual or smaller flower displays
- Namaqualand daisies, gousblom, gazania, vygies
- Scenic mountain pass, mountain views, photography, cycling, 4x4 routes, highlights of Caracal Eco Route: the historic Messelpad Pass with its masonry and the ruins where the prisoners were stationed while building the pass, at the base of the Buffels River Valley. The road to Soebatsfontein and Wallekraal is one of the most popular flower routes, travelling past a series of flower farms: Grootvlei, Skilpad, Bokskraal, Horees and Baksteenhoek

Wildeperdehoek Pass ('Wild horse corner' pass) is nearly inextricably linked to the Messelpad Pass and forms the passage over the mountains between Springbok and the West Coast. The pass is reputedly named because it was once a habitat for wild horses.

Both roads were constructed in the late 1860s by the engineer Patrick Fletcher and a group of prisoners from Cape Town. The ruins of the building where they were stationed at the base of the Buffels River valley still exist. The master dry-stone walls have been likened to the work of Thomas Bain. In a comparable vein, they stand nowadays as a testimony to excellent workmanship.

Wildeperdehoek Pass was an important transportation route for many years and a popular route for traders and explorers, who used it to transport goods and supplies across the region. It was the original route for transporting copper ore from the mines to Hondeklipbaai. When a transport upgrade for the mines became necessary in the mid-1860s, the Messelpad was embarked on, in 1866. But in 1869, work began on a railway from Port Nolloth. The Messelpad was not completed, and Port Nolloth took over from Hondeklipbaai as the shipping port for the mines. The pass is also known for its scenic beauty, with stunning views of the surrounding mountains and valleys.

Lapeirousia silenoides (endemic)

Kamieskroon

✱✱✱✱✱

- **Mid to end August**
- **Namaqualand daisies, gousblom, gazania, vygies, sporries, watsonias, kalkoentjie**
- **Gateway to Namaqualand flowers, hiking, cycling, birding, Namaqua landscapes**

Kamieskroon was founded in 1924, when the townspeople agreed the village of Bowesdorp had grown too large for its surroundings. Water scarcity forced the townspeople of Bowesdorp to uproot and plant themselves at the foothills of the Kamiesberge.

Although no one can agree on the name's derivation, Kamies may come from the Nama phrase 'kam', which indicates two, referring to the twin peaks topped with a vast, cleft rock a kilometre from the village. Some agree on the word kroon, which refers to the 'crown', a rather distinctive rocky peak that resembles the shape of a crown; others disagree with this and say the name Kamieskroon was given to the new village because the village itself was now 'the Crown of the Kamiesberg'.

Kamieskroon

Orange daisies at Grootvlei

Fields of knopiesopslag, Kamiesberg

Namaqua National Park (Skilpad Wildflower Reserve)

✳✳✳✳✳

- **Spectacular from mid to late August to September**
- **Namaqualand daisies, gousblom, gazania, vygies, sporries, surings, kalkoentjie, *Babiana* and many bulb species**
- **Spectacular wildflower displays, accommodation, hiking trails, scenic route, game viewing (small antelope), photography, birding, picnic spots**

The Skilpad farm was purchased by the World Wildlife Fund for Nature in 1988 to establish a wildflower reserve to preserve the land and its wildflowers. Skilpad, which translates as 'tortoise' in Afrikaans, is home to the Namaqua speckled tortoise, the smallest tortoise in the world. The farm was comprised mainly of shrubland and old wheat fields and was primarily used for livestock grazing, resulting in severe land degradation.

The farm was converted and the Namaqua National Park officially opened in 1999. Conservationists, led by Dr Karen Esler, recognised the area's ecological significance and began working to restore the land. The team implemented various conservation measures, including removing invasive plant species, controlling erosion and reintroducing indigenous plant species. Thanks to their efforts, the park has become a crucial conservation area, boasting diverse plant and animal life. The official proclamation of the Namaqua National Park's land occurred in 2002.

The reserve is situated on a ridge of hills about 700 m above sea level, so it receives more rain and mist than the surrounding areas. As a result, the park is a popular grazing area for sheep during the off-season, which helps to control weeds that would otherwise inhibit the growth of the annual daisies, resulting in a smaller variety of species but more dramatic colours.

These dry, dusty farmlands with tortured rock formations and big blue skies experience an almost reliable annual transformation, even in 'poor' flower seasons and their rolling hills are changed in waves of orange that bejewel the granite boulders of the Kamies mountains.

5 km scenic route

Fields of orange daisies, Namaqua National Park

White sporrie against a backdrop of orange daisies

A tapestry of knopiesopslag, orange daisies, Cape marigold, vygies, sambreeltjies, hongerblomme and sporrie, Soebatsfontein side of Namaqua National Park

Bowesdorp church ruins

Bowesdorp

- **Mid to end August; few flowers on average**
- **Namaqualand daisies, gazania, gousblom, vygies**
- **Village, scenic valley, rural experience, historical ruins of old church, old cars**

Established on the farm Wilgenhoutskloof, Bowesville – which later became Bowesdorp – was founded in a narrow rocky valley between high mountains near Kamieskroon. The town was named after Dr Henry Bowe, the district surgeon at the time, and the first Dutch Reformed Church in Namaqualand was built and completed in 1864.

In 1924, the church roof needed significant repairs, a reliable water source was scarce, and it was agreed the community had grown too large for its surroundings. The townspeople of Bowesdorp uprooted and planted themselves about 7 km south at Kamieskroon. The church and all the other buildings were left to the elements and time. Now, the discarded, crumbling constructions serve as reminders for us of human habitation.

Bowesdorp has many classic, old motors resting on the hard ground. Jannie van Niekerk, mechanic and owner of the land, leaves them there deserted and corroding in an informal scrapyard; a fascinating, spacious, outdoor morgue for old vintage motor cars.

Window into the past

Rooifontein quiver tree forest

- Late August to September; the quiver trees flower in May
- Quiver trees, succulents (various species), aloe, daisies, some small annuals
- Quiver tree photography, walks among quiver trees, stargazing, desert flora exploration

The vast and monotonous expanse of the Kamiesberg area gives the impression of a barren and lifeless environment. However, it is here that the ancient giants, formerly known as Aloe dichotoma and now referred to as Aloidendron dichotomum, find their habitat. These majestic trees possess crowns that are often compact and rounded in shape, a result of their branches repeatedly dividing into forks, which gives rise to their species name dichotoma, meaning 'forked'.

These trees evoke visions of a wild and primordial Africa, imbued with a survivor's spirit that shines like beaten copper. The Khoisan people roamed the region long before modern settlers traversed this land. They hollowed out the tree trunks and used them to store the day's hunting spoils. The trunk's rough, fibrous tissue helped to keep the meat cool as air flowed through it, acting as a natural refrigerator.

Carved and twisted by the sun and heat, these giants emerge with an upside-down appearance, their branches resembling roots. The harsh climatic conditions of the area have forced these aloes to adapt to survive, absorbing every drop of available water amid low soil moisture, air humidity and intense sunshine.

A donkey and bright gazania (botterblom) greet visitors

Rooifontein – Quiver tree forest

The massed array of *Felicia australis*, cheerful blue-mauve ray florets dancing in the breeze, makes a striking contrasting background to these carved and twisted giant quiver trees.

Kamassies

✱✱ – ✱✱✱✱✱

- **Late August; spectacular in good year**
- **Namaqualand daisies, gousblom, vygies, sporries**
- **Remote Namaqua area, scenic beauty, stargazing, photography, beautiful route with good flower displays, cycling**

Kamassies is a hamlet on a far-flung avenue northeast of Kamieskroon. The name Kamassies is derived from a Khoikhoi phrase, Kamiesberg se mase, which means 'the loveliness of the Kamiesberg'. The name is associated with the succulent vegetation abundant in the area, which has long been appreciated by the indigenous Khoikhoi people.

Splashes of yellow varkiesknolle (*Conicosia elongata*) on the sandy plains of Kamassies in the Kamiesberg

Mauve vygie bushes colour the arid veld of the Kamiesberg, near Kamassies

Bittergousblom, Kamassies

Karas

Late August

Namaqualand daisies, gousblom, vygies

Namaqua landscapes, rural charm, flower viewing (seasonal)

Nestled within the Kamiesberg mountains, Karas is in the heart of the Namaqualand region. This region is renowned for its breathtaking wildflower displays and forms part of a circular route showcasing the best of Namaqualand. Karas offers an unspoilt and rural experience, largely unaffected by the relentless march of progress.

Orange daisies stand out against the barren trees, Karas

Colchicum capense ssp. _ciliolatum_ – Kokerdoosblom, uilblaar

It is a charming sight as the late afternoon light slants through the pale, sail-like white flowers, looking like white butterflies gathering on the ground while the sunlight highlights their wings. These are the flowers after which Leliefontein was named. They are upright flowers found at the base of the bract and are usually green-white and egg-shaped. They form a cup that embraces the flowers, often referred to as a cup and saucer and are found in sandy, often moist places.

Leliefontein

- **Late August; little flowers; in a good year flowers around Leliefontein can be amazing**
- **Namaqualand daisies, gousblom, vygies, watsonias, the lilies of Leliefontein**
- **Historical mission station, church, Boer War history, Nama cultural experience, scenic mountain area**

Leliefontein, the oldest mission village in Namaqualand, traces its roots back to the kraal of a Nama chief named Jantjie Wildschut. In 1809, mission work began here under the London Missionary Society. However, the village was abandoned as a consequence of a troublesome attack by competing settlers in 1811. It was later revived by Reverend Barnabas Shaw, a Wesleyan minister, and a mission station was established in 1816 to spread Christianity among the local Khoisan people. It was named Leliefontein, meaning 'lily spring' in Afrikaans, possibly inspired by the abundance of white lilies and the natural spring there.

Over time, the mission station evolved into a settlement and, in 1818, the first church was constructed. This village became an important centre for the Dutch Reformed Church's missionary activities in the region. It also became a focal point for education, healthcare and social services for the local Khoisan population.

At present, Leliefontein is a small village with approximately 1 500 residents. Some families still reside in traditional *matjieshuise*, dome-shaped huts crafted from reed mats. The Nama community owns farmlands in the vicinity and many continue to use donkey carts for transportation. Its historic church, which withstood the ravages of the Anglo Boer War, was designated a national monument in 1980.

Garies

✱✱✱✱✱

- **From mid August; spectacular in a good season**
- **Namaqualand daisies, gousblom, gazania, vygies, sporries, kapokbos**
- **Get a marked map at Garies information centre with all the good flower spots up to Springbok (027 652 1220). A good base for exploring the surrounding areas including Namaqua National Park and Hondeklipbaai; cycling, hiking, scenic routes, Garies museum, rural town experience**

Garies was established on Goedeverwagting Farm, which its owner donated to the Dutch Reformed Church in 1845. Originally known as Th'aries by the Nama people, the area derived its name from the couch grass that grew alongside the stream's banks. Over time, the name, Th'aries was changed to Garies.

Today, Garies is a quaint agricultural village characterised by a long main street with a historic church constructed in the early 20th century, the old police station dating back to the colonial era, and a cluster of houses and retail outlets along the stream's banks.

The Khoikhoi people have inhabited this region for generations, and their rich culture and traditions remain integral to the town's identity. During the colonial era, Garies was an important centre of trade and commerce, serving as a vital transportation hub for goods and people between the coast and the interior.

The tulip, Moraea miniata, brightens up a kraal close to Garies

A quiver tree (*Aloidendron dichotomum*) stands proudly amid orange daisies and blougif (*Albuca cooperi*)

Bright orange daisies and yellow knopiesopslag line a road near Garies

A colourful array of wildflowers including yellow knopiesopslag, white sporrie, orange daisies and yellow and pink hongerblomme around the stone house near Garies

Wildflowers between Garies and Wallekraal, featuring yellow knopiesopslae, skilpadbos, gousblom, white sporrie, orange daisies and yellow and pink hongerblomme

Groenrivier

The Caracal Eco Route ✱✱ - ✱✱✱✱✱

◷ Mid to late August, little flowers on average, a lot in a good year

✱ Namaqualand daisies, gousblom, vygies, succulents (various species)

⚑ A 176–200 km 4x4 trail, starting in Namaqua National Park and ending at Groen River Mouth (6–8 hours). Includes diverse habitats, wildlife (caracal, other small predators, buck), scenic passes and coastal areas like the Groen River estuary. Get a route booklet from the Skilpad Rest Camp Office: 027 672 1948.

The Caracal Eco Route meanders along stunning landscapes encompassing various Namaqua environments, from the panoramic Kamiesberg with its boundless vistas to the awe-inspiring West Coast.

Setting out from the renowned Skilpad Wildflower Reserve, now a part of the Namaqua National Park, the route descends towards Soebatsfontein before veering northward to the verdant plains of Wildeperdehoek.

The road traverses the Namaqua flatlands, renowned for the unique Riethuis quartz and dry fynbos vegetation in the inland dune areas. As you cross the main Hondeklipbaai road, you enter the Namaqwa coastal section of the park, which boasts an impressive 50 km coastline, culminating at the mouth of the Groen River. This route covers approximately 250 km and treats visitors to a diverse tapestry of jagged mountains, expansive plains and glorious wildflowers.

The name Caracal Eco Route pays homage to the caracal, a small native wildcat that inhabits the region. While sightings of these elusive creatures are rare, lucky travellers may catch a fleeting glimpse as they navigate the rugged terrain of the Namaqualand area.

Perdeblom (*Didelta carnosa*), Groenrivier

Perdeblom (*Didelta carnosa*) at Groenrivier Lighthouse

Groenrivier

* - ***

- **Late August; little flowers, moderate in a good year**
- **Daisies, vygies, coastal fynbos species**
- **Coastal fishing, remote beach, camping, birding, stargazing**

Emerging from the Kamiesberg mountain range, the Groen River gracefully flows towards the Green River mouth lighthouse, where it meets the sea. Unfortunately, the lighthouse is currently inaccessible to visitors. The Groen River estuary stands out for its great salinity, making it one of the saltiest estuaries along the South African coast.

Along the Caracal Eco Route trail, you will encounter a series of secluded bays, including Boggerolbaai, Skiploodsbaai, Galjoenbaai, Koringkorrelbaai and Bleekskipbaai. The path leads you across the Bitter River, traversing white dunes, passing a seal colony and a freshwater fountain, and eventually arriving at the intriguing Spoegrivier caves.

The Bitter River dunes present an exceptional example of a dynamic and shifting dune system. As one of the few remaining pristine systems on the South African coast, they enjoy protection as a significant conservation feature of the park. The Groen River mouth signifies the conclusion of the Caracal Eco Route.

Perdeblom (*Didelta carnosa*)

Spoegrivier

- **Late August; patches of flowers, moderate in a good year**
- **Daisies, vygies, coastal fynbos species**
- **Caves (archaeological site), coastal scenery, fishing, remote beach, birding**

The coastline of the Groen and Spoeg rivers showcases untouched natural dune vegetation shielded from mining activities. This 50 km stretch of coastline, barring a solitary fountain, lacks fresh water. The presence of the cold Benguela current results in a regular mist, nourishing the unique plant communities.

The region's estuaries, marshlands and dunelands contribute to its profound conservation value. In 2008, De Beers Consolidated Mines made this land available, subsequently integrating it into the Namaqua National Park. The caves here hold historical and cultural significance, offering evidence of sheep farming practices dating back 2 000 years.

Rocky shores and seemingly endless stretches of white sandy beaches grace this beautiful coast, intermingled with picturesque little bays.

Strandlelie at the Spoegrivier caves

Spoegrivier

Bitterfontein

- **Mid to end of August**
- **Daisies, gousblom, vygies, succulents**
- **Railway junction, fuel stop, Namaqualand transition point, basic supplies, birdlife and home to martial eagles, Vanmeerhof Cave on the farm Meerhof, guided succulent plant tours, mountain biking, hiking**

Close to Bitterfontein

Renowned for its bitter-tasting, mineral-rich water, Bitterfontein became home to South Africa's first desalination plant in 1990, supplying clean water to the town's residents and the nearby community of Nuwerus. This remarkable achievement also marked the first-ever facility of its kind in the southern hemisphere.

Bitterfontein became significant in 1927, when the railway line from Cape Town extended there, facilitating the transportation of various goods, including green granite and copper ore extracted from the quarries and mines in the region. However, with ongoing development and road improvements, the influence of the railway station at Bitterfontein has waned. As a result, this nearly forgotten village on the fringes of the Western Cape has gradually faded into relative obscurity.

Bitterfontein

Daisies and *Lachenalias*, Bitterfontein

Nuwerus

- Some fields of flowers late August
- Namaqualand daisies, vygies
- Small agricultural village, overnight stop, basic amenities, Namaqualand landscape views

In the bygone era before motorised transportation took over, this tiny hamlet within the Hardeveld region was vital as a halfway station between Vanrhynsdorp and Garies. Given the long distance, a resting point was necessary for horses and riders to recuperate. Thus, Aardvarkgat, a station providing stables and a place of respite, was established. Over time, the name was changed to Nuwerus, meaning 'new rest'.

Nuwerus holds a delicate appeal that demands stillness and patience to fully appreciate its hidden beauty. Life here follows the rhythm set by nature rather than human development. Though modest in size, the village's significance lies in its location within the succulent Karoo biome, which harbours numerous plant species found nowhere else.

Roadside gazania

Spring blooms transform the once barren patches of soil, also called heuweltjies, into breathtaking flower displays, near Soebatsfontein

Vygies explode in a riot of bright pink, near Bagdad Café

Knersvlakte

August; patches of wildflowers

Vygies, daisies, various succulents, dwarf succulent annuals

Karoo biome exploration, unique plant species (endemic), scenic drives, photography (especially for botanists), stargazing

The Knersvlakte lies between Vanrhynsdorp and Vredendal, stretching across a desolate and monotonous landscape north of the Olifants River. This region is notorious for its harsh climate, meagre rainfall and abundant small, white, coarse quartz stones with sparse vegetation.

The name Knersvlakte can be attributed to various interpretations. One theory suggests it stems from the sound produced by ox wagon wheels as early settlers traversed the quartzite gravel, resembling a grinding or gnashing noise. Another explanation proposes it symbolises the determination of the pioneers who braved the journey across the country, as captured in the saying: "Dit kos tande kners om die vlakte oor te steek," (It takes gritting on your teeth to cross the plain), highlighting the arduousness of the terrain and their resolute spirit.

Remarkably, hidden among the bleakness, delicate dwarf succulents, like the endearingly named bababoudjies ('baby bums'), thrive in this inhospitable environment. They grow amid striking rock formations, creating a captivating contrast against the snow-like quartzite. These plants have adapted to survive by making use of the sunlight reflected off the white quartzite, which prevents them from overheating, as they would in an environment of darker rocks and soil.

Despite the threats posed by desertification, overgrazing, poaching and climate change, Namaqualand's semi-arid regions possess a unique landscape characterised by their otherworldly beauty and charm.

Stone plant (*Argyroderma* sp.)

Stone plant (*Argyroderma* sp.)

Knersvlakte

The landscape is dominated by vygies, members of the family Aizoacea (*Mesembryanthemoidea*), particularly the distinctive bababoudjies. These dwarf succulents, resembling pebbles, are strategically scattered across the quartz gravel. Their silvery-green or grey leaves reflect sunlight, while their purple or yellow flowers add a splash of colour during the autumn and winter.

The hygrochastical fruiting capsules, characteristic of the vygie family (Aizoaceae, Mesembryanthemoidea), have a number of valves (locules), which open when wet to disperse the seeds, and close again when dry, ensuring the next generation of these resilient plants.

Vast stretches of the Knersvlakte are covered in small, rough white quartz stones, with only a scattering of vegetation

Vanrhynsdorp

- Spectacular mid to late August to September; contact the tourism office during flower season for latest flower information
- Namaqualand daisies, gousblom, gazania, vygies, sporries, bulbinella and many bulbs
- Latsky radio museum, Namaqua wagon museum, Kokerboom nursery, wine tasting, stargazing

In 1661, Pieter van Meerhoff, a Danish traveller, initially explored the Knersvlakte area near Vanrhynsdorp. In 1874, the Troe-Troe Mission Congregation was founded. Subsequently, various mission stations were established, eventually evolving into towns.

The Dutch Reformed Church's congregation gathered at the Troe-Troe homestead, which can still be seen here.

Nestled in a remote setting, this town radiates Victorian charm. In 1881, the town underwent a name change. It became Vanrhynsdorp to honour Petrus Benjamin van Rhyn, a prominent individual in the community who made significant contributions as a church leader and active member.

Vanrhynsdorp, a key regional business hub, is the gateway to Namaqualand, offering access to the Hantam Karoo, the Knersvlakte succulents and the Cederberg. It also plays a vital role in supporting the extensive sheep farming district. The local succulent nursery has gained international acclaim for its exceptional cultivation and care of native succulents, establishing itself as a leader in its field.

Namaqualand daisy (*Dimorphotheca spp.*)

Vanrhynsdorp

Orange daisies blanket the sidewalks

Beetle daisies get their name from the dark specks that mimic beetles

Maskam

- Mid to late August to September; spectacular in good year
- Namaqualand daisies, gousblom, gazania, vygies, sporries, disas (in wetter areas), babianas and many bulbs
- Hiking and mountain biking, birding, photography

The guest farm, Maskam, takes its name from the Khoikhoi word Matsikamma, which means 'place of water'.

The farm boasts various flower species in spring against a beautiful mountain backdrop. While the density of flowers fluctuates with rainfall, the diversity is impressive.

Unlike national parks, where walking among the flowers is strictly prohibited, this is a private working farm. Visitors are welcome to explore the flowers on foot or by vehicle. A high-clearance vehicle is recommended for driving the 5.6 km trail and 7.8 km trail.

White, yellow and orange daisies, froetangs, gansogies and lazy daisies have reclaimed the old rooibos tea plantation

Orange daisies with the Gifberg mountain towering in the distance, Maskam farm

Bright yellow brakslaai, Maskam

Veldkool blossoms among a soft backdrop of lazy daisies (*Foveolina tenella*)

White, orange and yellow daisies light up the field at Maskam

Gifberg spoelgat at Gifberg holiday farm

The ruins at Nieuwoudtville with a cheerful display of orange daisies

Nieuwoudtville

and Hantam Karoo

NIEUWOUDTVILLE AND HANTAM KAROO

Centuries before the arrival of the first settlers around 1730, the Khoisan people inhabited this area, leaving a lasting cultural legacy. The rock art found in the Oorlogskloof Nature Reserve and on farms surrounding Nieuwoudtville is a testament to the flourishing ancient culture that once thrived here. The early settlers chose to establish themselves near the present-day town of Nieuwoudtville, specifically at Groenrivier and Willemsrivier, where the remnants of the first formal church building still stand.

In 1897, the town of Nieuwoudtville was officially founded on land purchased from HC Nieuwoudt, the individual after whom it was named. The town's impressive old buildings were constructed from sandstone, and many of these architectural gems have withstood the test of time, still gracing the town today.

During the Boer War, which erupted in 1899, evidence of skirmishes can be found throughout the region, and local residents hold colourful stories of the war, passed down through generations.

Situated in the Hantam Karoo, Nieuwoudtville rests peacefully on the serene Bokkeveld Plateau, named after the once-abundant herds of zebra, wildebeest and springbok that roamed the area.

During the flowering season, the convergence of Cape fynbos, mountain Renosterveld and succulent Karoo biomes enhances the region's natural splendour. With over 1 350 plant species, the inhabitants of this historic settlement proudly refer to it as the 'bulb capital of the world', captivating visitors from far and wide.

The April fool or skeerkwas (*Haemanthus coccineus*), emerges from the tough soil, Boereplaas

A fiery display of katsterte (*Red Bulbinella*), Boereplaas

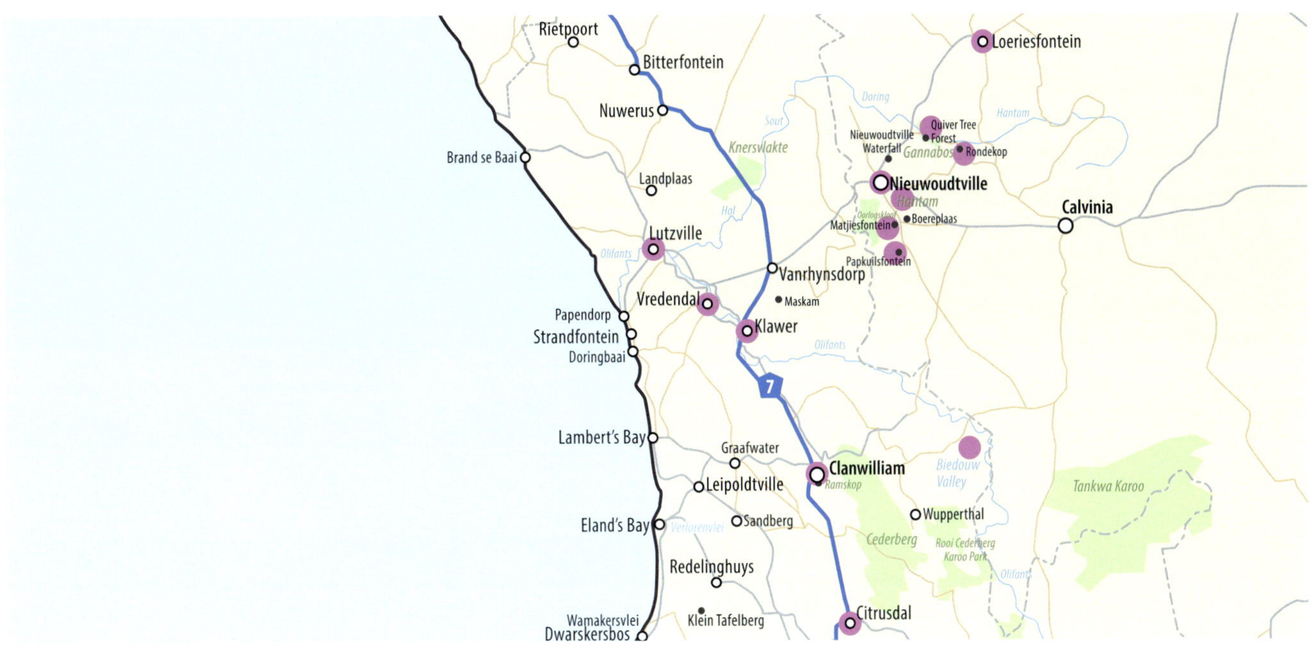

Red cup and saucer (*Colchicum burchellii* subsp. *pulchrum*), Matjiesfontein

Quick facts about Nieuwoudtville

The Nieuwoudtville area in the **Northern Cape** province of South Africa transforms into a vibrant floral wonderland during spring. The area is on the **Bokkeveld Plateau**, where the vegetation is a unique combination of **fynbos**, **succulent Karoo** and **Renosterveld**. The area is a biodiversity hotspot, often called the **Bulb Capital of the World** since it includes thousands of **geophytes** (bulbous plants). Daisies and other rare species also abound.

Why the area is great for bulbous plants

Geology, topography, soils and climate determine the biodiversity of an area.

- The Nieuwoudtville area is on the **Bokkeveld Plateau**, which is geologically distinct and ancient.
- **Bokkeveld shale** is a soft sedimentary rock that weathers into **fertile, clay-rich soils that hold water well**. These conditions are crucial for bulbs that need moisture in the short, wet season.
- In some areas, intrusions of dolerite (a volcanic rock) contribute to **mineral-rich soils** and add variation in soil chemistry and drainage.
- In surrounding areas, **sandstone ridges** add to topographic and ecological diversity, supporting a mosaic of vegetation types.
- The **plateau structure** is a relatively flat or gently rolling landscape, around 750–850 m above sea level.
- This elevation results in **cooler temperatures** and **more rainfall** than the surrounding lowlands – a rare advantage in this semi-arid region.

Top places to explore

- **Hantam National Botanical Garden:** Trails and rich diversity; renosterbos, fynbos and dolomite koppies. Rare endemic bulbs include Romulea, Moraea and Lachinalia.
- **Nieuwoudtville Wild Flower Reserve:** Dense blooms and easy access. Encompasses critically endangered Hantam-Roggeveld dolerite Renosterveld.
- **Road to Loeriesfontein:** Roadside flower carpets.
- **Matjiesfontein Farm:** Biodiverse private farm. Picturesque setting, 7 km self-drive loop through flower fields.
- **Ramskop Nature Reserve:** In Clanwilliam, 2 km circular footpath. It is a focal point for conservation.

Biodiversity

Nieuwoudtville is a **geophyte heaven**, home to hundreds of species, some **endemic**, meaning they grow nowhere else on Earth. Nieuwoudtville is not purely about flowers – it's a full-on biodiversity hotspot with fascinating wildlife. The **Bokkeveld Plateau** is home to plenty of **mammals**, **reptiles**, **birds** and **insects**, many of which are specially adapted to the semi-arid environment.

Botanical richness

- Slight **slope**, **aspect and soil depth** variations across the plateau create **microhabitats** supporting incredible plant diversity.
- The seasonal rainfall pattern of **cool, wet winters** and **hot, dry summers** is perfect for bulbs. They store energy underground during summer dormancy and burst into bloom after rain.
- **Clay-rich** soils hold moisture long enough for bulbs to grow, but not so much that they rot.
- Bulbs thrive in places with **natural** or **occasional disturbance** (like grazing or fire), and the open, low-competition habitats of Nieuwoudtville suit them well.
- The area has remained ecologically stable over **millions of years**, giving time for incredible **speciation and endemism** among bulbous plants; think *Lachenalia*, *Romulea*, *Babiana*, *Moraea*, **Gladiolus**, *Geissorhiza*, *Ferraria* and more.
- **Annual herbs** and **wildflowers** are short-lived but spectacular in springtime. They germinate quickly after winter rains and flower for a few weeks in spring.

Animal biodiversity

- **Insects and pollinators** include monkey beetles, carpenter bees, bee flies, hoverflies, butterflies and antlions.
- **Amphibians and reptiles** include rain frogs, Cape sand snakes, puff adders, boomslangs, padloper tortoises, armoured agamas and others.
- **Birds** include the blue crane, Ludwig's bustard, Cape eagle-owl, malachite sunbird, Karoo lark, Cape bunting, Namaqua sandgrouse and other dryland specialists.
- **Mammals** include shy and nocturnal bat-eared foxes, Cape foxes, porcupines and aardvark. Small antelope such as steenbok and grey duiker and dassies (hyraxes) are common.

Nieuwoudtville Wildflower Reserve

✱✱✱✱✱

- **Spectacular in March and mid to late July to September; contact the tourism office for the latest flower information and map**
- **Sparaxis, *Lachenalia*, *Babiana*, gladiolus, *Ixia*, *Geissorhiza*, Namaqualand daisies, gousblom, vygies, sporries (*Heliophila variabilis*), candelabra lilies, cat's tails (*Bulbinella*), hongerblom (*Senecio*), suring (*Oxalis sonderiana*), sambreeltjies (*Felicia*)**
- **Walking trails, cycling routes, birding and wildflower route**

The 115 hectare Nieuwoudtville Wildflower Reserve, situated 3 km east of Nieuwoudtville, boasts over 300 indigenous flora species, including the rare red cat's tail (*Bulbinella* sp.).

Once inside, the road branches into two roughly 2 km loops. Further along, you will reach a circular area behind some rocks, perfect for parking and climbing to a scenic lookout point. The sweet-smelling air, buzzing bees and breathtaking views create a serene atmosphere.

Visitors can drive close to the flowers, immersing themselves in their beauty. The reserve also features a variety of bulbs and a short hiking trail winding between rock formations, revealing even more hidden floral treasures. The unique blend of vibrant colours truly sets this wildflower reserve apart.

The name of the bokhorinkie (*Diascia namaquensis*) is inspired by its likeness to a buck, complete with horns

Nieuwoudtville Wildflower Reserve in full bloom, showcasing yellow katsterte, daisies, hongerblomme and delicate white flax

Candelabra lily, Boereplaas

Brunsvigia bosmaniae

In Nieuwoudtville, autumn brings a unique floral show with the candelabra lily/Maartblom (*Brunsvigia bosmaniae*). Like other plants in the amaryllis family, the candelabra lily grows from a bulb. This underground bulb helps the plant survive long, dry periods, ready to burst into life when autumn rains arrive. Modest rain in March is enough to trigger these magnificent blooms. Within weeks the landscape is covered in countless pink, trumpet-shaped flowers that form striking, candelabra-like heads. These vibrant clusters stand out dramatically against the rugged dolerite hills and soft granite sands.

Once the candelabra lily flowers fade, they focus on producing seeds. The whole dried flower head often breaks off and tumbles across the land like a tumbleweed, scattering seeds far and wide.

Candelabra lily or Maartblom (*Brunsvigia bosmaniae*), Nieuwoudtville Wildflower Reserve

Blue sambreeltjies, bluebells (*Ixia*) and pink hongerblomme, Hantam National Botanical Garden

Hantam National Botanical Garden

- **August to September**
- ***Lapeirousia oreogena*, *Sparaxis elegans*, *Hyacinthaceae*, *Iridaceae* and *Amarylidaceae* plant families**
- **Walking trails, diverse range of bulbs and wildflowers**

The Hantam National Botanical Garden at Nieuwoudtville is South Africa's ninth national botanical garden and the only one in the Northern Cape. This unique gem boasts an astonishing diversity of flora, with a remarkable 1 350 plant species identified within its boundaries.

While spring is renowned for its floral displays, autumn can also unveil surprises. A mere 23 mm of March rainfall at the Hantam Botanical Garden is sufficient to trigger the spectacular blooming of *Brunsvigia bosmaniae*, affectionately known as the Maartblom or March flower/lily.

Within weeks, the landscape transforms as countless, pink, trumpet-shaped flowers emerge, adorning the dolerite koppies. These striking blooms, clustered in round candelabra-like heads, create a breathtaking contrast against the granite sands.

Yellow katstert (*Bulbinella* sp.)

White and yellow daisies, yellow and pink hongerblomme and delicate white flax are highlights at Hantam Botanical Garden

Yellow daisies on the ± 7 km circular flower route at Matjiesfontein

Matjiesfontein Farm

- **August to September**
- **Gladiolus splendens, African daisies, satynblom, pietsnot, sterretjies, candelabra lilies**
- **7 km wildflower route, hiking trails, traditional boerekos at Matjiesfontein farm stall**

The farm Matjiesfontein, 14 km south of Nieuwoudtville, boasts one of the world's most diverse collections of wildflowers.

The owners of the land allow their sheep to graze on the dried flowers. Combined with the sheep manure and scattered seeds, this natural process of disturbing the soil prepares the land for the next growth cycle, ensuring future generations can continue to marvel at this breathtaking show.

Embark on a scenic 7 km circular drive through fields ablaze with yellow daisies. This vibrant display is a short-lived spectacle, as the flowers soon succumb to the arid landscape.

Nemesia or kappieblommetjie

Papkuilsfontein Flower Route

✱✱✱ – ✱✱✱✱✱

August to September

Katsterte, rain daisies, yellow daisies, satyn blomme, pers sambreeltjies

Situated on the farm Papkuilsfontein, 23 km south of Nieuwoudtville, the route is only 3 km but has many flowers and bulbs. Get a map at Waenhuis restaurant on Papkuilsfontein farm.

Rondekop/Naressie Route

✱✱✱ – ✱✱✱✱✱

August to September

White flax, yellow and orange daisies and hongerblomme

This 42 km circular route offers a Karoo-like landscape, with expansive fields of daisies, sporrie and vygies. The colourful scenery is truly breathtaking, almost like a painting coming to life.

Papkuilsfontein

Rondekop/Naressie Route

Yellow katsterte (*Bulbinella* sp.), Papkuilsfontein

Gannabos quiver tree forest

- **End of August; few flower displays; the quiver trees flower in May**
- **Quiver trees (kokerboom), succulents (various species), aloe, some small annuals**
- **Photography, walks/hikes, stargazing**

Located near Loeriesfontein stands a remarkable natural marvel: one of South Africa's largest colonies of giant aloes known as Aloidendron dichotomum. These tree-like aloe plants primarily thrive on warm north-facing slopes and have lifespans exceeding 300 years. Bushmen hollowed out the branches, giving the tree its name, to fashion quivers for their arrows. These skilled hunters relied on lightly constructed bows and arrows that are not powerful enough to subdue or kill large prey immediately. To enhance their hunting prowess, they applied potent poisons to their arrows, derived from various sources, including plants, snakes and insects. By combining their skill in archery with the power of these natural poisons, the San developed a highly effective hunting strategy that sustained them for generations.

The quiver tree leaves also treat various ailments, including stomach disorders and skin infections and the sap is used as glue.

With stems reaching heights up to 4 m and boasting a distinct cylindrical shape, the quiver tree stores water in its succulent trunk and branches, enabling survival in hot and arid conditions. Certain branches are strategically sacrificed to endure excessive water stress by cutting off the water flow. Fallen trees result from old age or drought and powerful winds that uproot them, and gradually they decay into inclined skeletons.

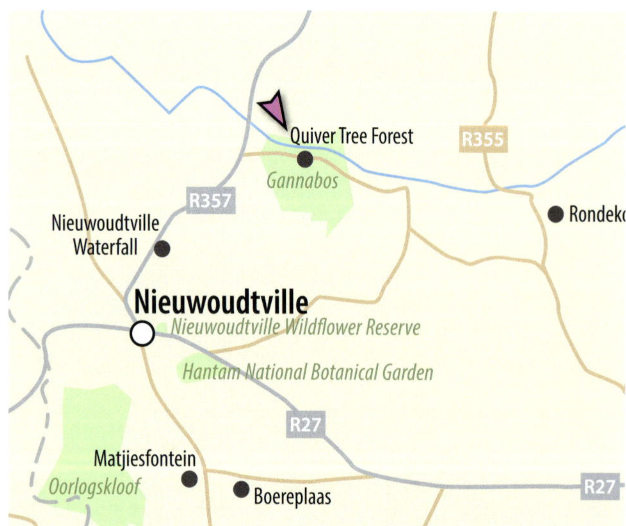

Flower buds of the quiver tree

Yellow duifiedoring (*Tribulus zeyheri*) spreads across the dry ground to the quiver trees, at Gannabos, near Loeriesfontein

Vygies and quiver trees, Gannabos

Loeriesfontein

✱✱✱ – ✱✱✱✱✱

- Mid to late August
- Namaqualand daisies, gousblom, vygies, sporries, bulbous plants
- Fred Turner museum, windmill museum, quiver tree forest (nearby), visit the Knersvlakte

Tucked away in a fold of hills on the northern slopes of the Skurweberg. Despite its isolation, the town gradually grew around a trading store established in 1894.

The village exudes a distinct charm, highlighted by the prominent presence of the Dutch Reformed Church in its Art Deco architectural style from the 1930s and a unique exhibit of 27 giant flower-like windmills firmly rooted within the grounds of the Fred Turner Museum. The museum showcases a collection of windmills, providing visitors with an intriguing glimpse into the history and technology of these remarkable structures. The windmills hail from distant locations, including the United States and Canada. As you wander through this display, you will be fascinated by the intricate construction and the impressive size of the windmill blades, meticulously designed to harness even the gentlest breezes.

The concept of the Windmill Museum originated from the late Dr Walton, a Cape Town resident from the United Kingdom. His passion for preserving South Africa's windmills led to the establishment of this extraordinary exhibit within the Fred Turner Museum's premises.

The Fred Turner Folk and Culture Museum is a treasure trove that celebrates the history of Loeriesfontein and its people and offers a glimpse into its rich heritage.

The etymology of the town's name remains uncertain, speculated to be inspired by the Knysna loerie bird, despite the species not inhabiting the area. Alternatively, it could be linked to a Jewish peddler named Lurie or derived from the Afrikaans term *loer*, meaning 'to peek'.

Nieuwoudtville waterfall

Fred Turner windpump museum

Road to Loeriesfontein

Klawer

Mid to late August

Namaqualand daisies, gousblom, vygies, gazanias, riverine annuals

Wine tasting, citrus tours (seasonal), Olifants River activities

The town owes its name to the abundant wild clover that blankets the surrounding area. The landscape features rolling hills adorned with fertile farmland and riverbanks set against dry, sparse scrubland.

The local economy thrives on table grape farming, which flourishes thanks to the Olifants-River Irrigation Scheme that supplies water to the surrounding farms, vineyards, orchards and fields.

The introduction of the railway in 1914 sparked a surge in agricultural endeavours, turning Klawer into a bustling centre of commerce with its newfound status as the then-final stop on the rail link connecting Cape Town and the Namaqua West Coast. This status as the last stop persisted for a decade, shaping Klawer's trajectory.

Mauve vygies on the Cape lime road towards Vredendal

Yellow hongerblomme in the orchard

Yellow, white and orange daisies, gazanias and vygies, Kleinberg

Clanwilliam

- Late August; surrounding areas like Rietfontein and the Biedouw Valley have spectacular flower displays
- Daisies, gousblom, vygies, fynbos species (proteas, ericas, restios in surrounding mountains), gladiolus
- Rooibos tea tasting and tours, Clanwilliam Dam, Cederberg rock art, Old Jail museum, hiking and mountain biking

Initially the town was laid out on the farm of Jan Disselsvlei. However, in 1814, the Governor of the Cape Colony, John Cradock, renamed the town in honour of his father-in-law, Richard Meade, the first Earl of Clanwilliam, who was also the serving governor at that time, and adopted the name Clanwilliam.

In 1930, Dr Pieter le Fras Nortier, a botanist, former Rhodes scholar and medical professional serving as a district surgeon, began experimenting with cultivating rooibos plants. Rooibos, a one-of-a-kind herbal tea endemic to the area, was becoming known for its remarkable health benefits. Recognising the tea's commercial potential for the region, Dr Nortier pioneered its cultivation on his farms, Eastside and Klein Kliphuis, in Clanwilliam.

Clanwilliam was an important centre of commerce and trade for the surrounding area, which remains a cornerstone of the town's economy today.

White daisies are reclaiming the unplanted land near Clanwilliam

White, orange and yellow daisies at Rietvlei

White, orange and yellow daisies in old rooibos field

Yellow daisies at Rietvlei

White rain daisies and yellow Namaqualand daisies

Ramskop Nature Reserve

- **Mid to end August**
- **Daisies, gousblom, gazania, vygies, various cultivated and indigenous annuals and perennials**
- **Cultivated wildflower garden with views overlooking the Clanwilliam Dam; braai and picnic spots, birding**

Ramskop Nature Reserve, also known as the Wildflower Garden, showcases an extensive collection of over 350 cultivated wildflower species. The reserve offers scenic walks along well-designed paths, providing breathtaking views of Clanwilliam Dam and the majestic Cederberg mountains.

Typical daisy composite structure with ray florets surrounding the central disc florets

Biedouw Valley

✱✱ - ✱✱✱

- **Later in August there are spectacular displays in a good year**
- **Namaqualand daisies, gousblom, gazania, vygies, everlastings, red crassula, gladiolus**
- **Scenic drives, photography, hiking, farm stays**

Its name derived from the indigenous plant 'biedou' or 'bietou', the Biedouw Valley delights visitors with its stunning natural beauty. A winding gravel pass connects this fertile valley to the farms at higher altitudes in the south and east.

Local farmers refrain from grazing their livestock in the valley during the flowering season to preserve this awe-inspiring spectacle. After abundant winter rainfall, the usually dry Agter-Pakhuis region transforms into an arresting display of spring flowers, enchanting the senses and imaginations of countless visitors.

The Biedouw Valley is known for its wide array of bulbous flowers. Yellow-and-white *Nemesia* nestles alongside blue *Heliophila*, gazania, mauve *Senecio*, *Lachenalia*, *Babiana*, *Ixia* and an array of succulent vygies that are seen in great profusion.

Flower field close to Enjo farm

Combination of flowers in the Biedouw Valley

Fields of orange and yellow daisies, Biedouw Valley

Citrusdal

- **Mid to late August**
- **Namaqualand daisies, gousblom, vygies, riverine annuals, fynbos species**
- **Hot springs, citrus farm tours (seasonal), hiking and mountain biking, wine tasting, Olifants River**

Nestled on the fertile banks of the Olifants River, Citrusdal derives its name from the principal agricultural activity of citrus farming in the area.

In 1916, the Dutch Reformed Church established a presence in Citrusdal to serve the residents of the Olifants River valley near the Cederberg mountains. The church acquired a portion of Middelpost farm, which was used to found a township to cater to the growing community.

Fields of dasies, Citrusdal

Fields of daisies

Among the citrus grove, Citrusdal

White rain daisy, Citrusdal

Vredendal

- Mid to late August
- Daisies, gousblom, vygies, riverine annuals
- Wine tasting, Olifants River wine route, museum, birding, agricultural tours

Situated near the southern border of the Namaqualand region, this delightful town was initially called Bakkeley Plaats, derived from Dutch and meaning 'battle farm', owing to a clash between Dutch settlers and the Khoikhoi in 1668. Subsequently, a peace agreement resolved the conflicts, leading to the town being renamed Vreedendaal, signifying the 'Valley of peace' in Dutch. Over time, it evolved into Vredendal and was carefully planned in 1933 as part of the Olifants River Irrigation Scheme, using the abundant waters from the Olifants River.

This irrigation system facilitated extensive agriculture and viticulture, creating a fertile, lush valley. The area boasts South Africa's most comprehensive wine cellar and numerous boutique wineries and dried fruit depots.

The town has grown from an original section of the Vredendal farm, which dates back to 1748, to serve as the administrative and commercial centre along the fertile banks of the Olifants River.

Vredendal enjoys a breathtaking backdrop comprising the magnificent peaks of Gifberg, Maskam and Koebee. Its landscapes blend contrastingly, including sandy plains, rugged mountains and a remarkable diversity of succulent plant species unique to the region.

Orange daisies cover the railway tracks, Kleinrivier Bridge, Vredendal

Vineyards are framed by brilliant pink vygies

Lutzville

Mid to late August

Daisies, gousblom, vygies, viooltjies

Wine tasting, agricultural exploration, fishing, birding, proximity to the coast

Nestled alongside the serene banks of the Olifants River, the village came into existence with the name Vleermuijsklip, bestowed by Pieter van Everaert in 1661. This notable rocky outcrop provided shelter to early travellers and was home to bats. In the middle of the 20th century, it was changed to Vlermuisklip and renamed in 1923 to honour its founder, John Lutz, an accomplished irrigation engineer who played a vital role in constructing the Clanwilliam Dam. Not only did Lutz contribute to the dam project, but he also conducted significant surveys of the Lutzville region, paving the way for agricultural expansion.

During high tide, one can navigate a light flat-bottomed boat downstream for approximately 30 km to Papendorp, near the river mouth. With fertile soils and a favourable climate, the region has become a treasured destination for winemakers who have adorned the landscape with picturesque vineyards, offering breathtaking views as their backdrop.

Gazanias splash the roadside with colour

Vast numbers of viooltjies (*Lachenalia*) colour the dull soil

Kelkiewyn (*Geissorhiza radians*), Waylands Flower Reserve, Darling

West Coast

of the Western Cape

WEST COAST OF THE WESTERN CAPE

The Atlantic Ocean bounds the rugged coastline to the west, the rolling wheat fields and vineyards of the Swartland to the east, and the fertile Olifants River valley to the north.

The remote landscape is thinly populated, with fertile fishing grounds, misty hills, estuaries and rivers. Characterised by desolate landscapes, with understated, yet compelling, vistas teeming with a diverse range of flora and fauna.

Evidence of human habitation has been unearthed in archaeological sites throughout the region, and the Khoikhoi people were the first to call it home. In the 17th century, the West Coast became a bustling trading post for goods. It also played a crucial role in expanding the fishing industry in South Africa. Today, the South African West Coast remains a culturally significant area, shaped by its past and its residents' unique way of life.

Nestled along the coast, charming fishing villages and historic towns provide a glimpse into the region's rich heritage. Residents are known for their love of seafood delicacies like snoek, mussels, crayfish and bokkoms. Nature lovers and hikers visit the area to spot migrating birds and whales.

The Cape and Karoo regions are the oldest centres of endemism, home to many plants and animals unique to these regions. Springtime brings abundant flowers in a riot of colours, filling the landscape with their beauty. The meadows are awash in brilliant red poppies, while the shimmering petals of vygies glint in the sun. As the day turns twilight, the land cools and a soft blue mist blankets the landscape, illuminating the white and yellow flowers like stars in the night sky.

Sea pumpkin (*Arctotheca populifolia*) at the Stompneus Point Lighthouse, Shelley Point

Yellow and pink hongerblomme, patches of blue sporrie, vygies and a dash of white and orange daisies, Langebaan Lagoon area

Quick facts about the West Coast of the Western Cape

The West Coast floral region in the Western Cape Province stretches from just north of Cape Town up towards Namaqualand. The vegetation of this area explodes into bloom every year after good winter rains, transforming its semi-arid landscape into a kaleidoscope of wildflowers. This region forms part of the **Cape Floristic Region**, one of Earth's **richest and most unique plant kingdoms**.

Why the area is great for ephemeral spring flowering plants

Geology, topography, soils and climate determine the biodiversity of an area.

- Underlying the West Coast are **ancient granites**, **shales** and **sandstone**, often overlain by wind-blown sands (dunes and Strandveld), **limestone ridges**, **coastal calcretes** and **tertiary marine deposits**.
- Soils are **nutrient-poor**, **sandy** and **well drained**, which reduces competition and favours specialised, slow-growing plants.
- The region is **gently undulating**, with **low hills**, **coastal plains** and **dune systems**.
- Drainage is patchy, creating **seasonal wetlands**, **vernal pools** and **gravel pans**, ideal for ephemeral spring flowers.
- **Open, unshaded landscapes** allow low-growing plants to maximise sunlight during their short flowering window.
- The **Mediterranean climate's** cool, moist winters enable underground bulbs and seeds to germinate. Dry summers force dormancy, conserving resources.
- Many species are **geophytes** (bulbous or tuberous), perfectly adapted to survive harsh summers underground.
- Plants are triggered by warming temperatures and soil moisture to **flower rapidly**, ensuring pollination before the summer heat.
- Small changes in slope, soil depth or exposure support an **incredible diversity of species**, many of which are endemic.

Top places to explore

- **West Coast National Park and Potsberg:** Unique and diverse habitats of Langebaan Lagoon, salt marshes, wetlands, coastal strip, seabirds, lowland fynbos, etc.
- **Tienie Versfeld Wildflower Reserve:** Situated near Darling, it is a botanical gem that conserves critically endangered Renosterveld and Swartland granite fynbos.
- **Langebaan:** Rich in fynbos, Strandveld and wetland flora.
- **Darling:** This is where small-town meets floral splendour; Renosterveld and Sandveld.
- **Jacobsbaai:** Between Saldanha and Vredenburg; Strandveld vegetation.

Biodiversity

The biodiversity of the West Coast of the Western Cape is globally exceptional, even within the famously rich Cape Floristic Region. Therefore, it is a **Global Biodiversity hotspot**. The **Cape Floristic Region** is one of only **six floral kingdoms in the world**, it is the **smallest but richest per unit area**. It contains **thousands of plant species**, with an extremely **high rate of endemism** (many species appear nowhere else on Earth).

Botanical richness

- **Over 1200 plant species** occur in places like the West Coast National Park alone.
- Dominated by **Renosterveld**, **sand fynbos** and **Strandveld**, all rich in **bulbs and geophytes**, e.g. *Babiana*, *Moraea*, *Lachenalia*; **daisy species** (*Asteraceae*) such as *Arctotis*, *Ursinia*, *Dimorphotheca*; **succulents** like vygies (*Aizoaceae, Mesembryanthemoidea*).
- Many plants are **adapted to drought, fire and seasonal moisture**, making them masters of survival and rapid blooming.
- Many habitats, like **sand fynbos**, are **critically endangered** as a result of agriculture, development and invasive species.
- The spring flower season provides a **brief glimpse** into an ancient and threatened ecosystem, often visible for only a few weeks each year.

Animal biodiversity

- **Insects and pollinators** include monkey beetles (important for daisy pollination), long-tongued flies, sunbirds and bees for tubular or nectar-rich flowers. It is interesting to know the complex plant-pollinator relationships drive co-evolution and species radiation.
- **Amphibians** appear during winter and spring.
- **Reptiles** include tortoises, such as the angulate tortoise.
- The wetland systems attract migratory **birds** during winter and spring.
- **Mammals** that can be spotted are small predators like bat-eared foxes, caracals and Cape foxes. Antelope include bontebok, springbok and eland.

The landscape at Postberg Nature Reserve is awash with white and orange daisies.

Ganzekraal

Mid to late September to October

Coastal fynbos species, dune fynbos, annuals (smaller quantities)

Camping, fishing, coastal walks, birding

Ganzekraal, a farm with roots dating back to the early 1700s, played a significant role in the Groene Kloof area. It is essential as part of the network of farms and outposts that extended under the Dutch East India Company (VOC) control from the Castle of Good Hope in Cape Town to Saldanha Bay.

Having been granted to Jacob van Reenen by a grateful government, Ganzekraal became one of the earliest freehold farms at the Cape. Jacob earned this recognition for his long and challenging journey to locate the wreck of the *Grosvenor*, which had been shipwrecked in 1782 on the North Transkei Wild Coast. The slave bell tower, still standing today, serves as a reminder of this expedition. It housed the bell retrieved from the *Grosvenor* wreck in 1790.

The exact origin of the name Ganzekraal remains uncertain, but it is believed to have derived from Dutch, referring to a 'goose enclosure' or 'place where geese are kept'. It is thought to have been named after a nearby farm or kraal where geese were raised by the original Dutch settlers in the region. While efforts have been made to restore some structures, only a few buildings have withstood the test of time.

Today, Ganzekraal attracts visitors as a popular destination for fishing, birding and various outdoor activities.

Arum lily

Despite its common name, arum lily, the *Zantedeschia aethiopica* is neither an arum nor a lily. However, its association with the lily as a symbol of purity remains strong. This elegant, faintly scented flower, with its distinctive arrowhead-shaped leaves, attracts a variety of pollinators and, in some regions, it even provides a habitat for the tiny Hyperolius hopstocki frog, which is endemic to South Africa. After flowering, the spathe turns green to protect the ripening berries. Once ripe, the succulent yellow berries attract birds, aiding seed dispersal.

A unique adaptation of the arum lily's leaves is guttation, which allows them to release excess water through specialised stomata. This mechanism prevents waterlogging and enables the plant to thrive in wet conditions.

It can grow to heights of 0.6-1 m but can reach even greater heights depending on the shade it receives. The plant may exhibit evergreen or deciduous behaviour, adjusting to the prevailing rainfall patterns. The flowering period typically occurs between August and January, though sporadic blooms can appear throughout the year. Here it rises over the horizon at Ganzekraal.

White arum lilies (*Zantedeschia aethiopica*) stand tall at Ganzekraal

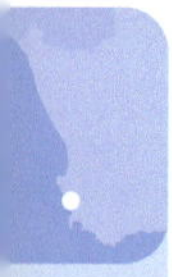

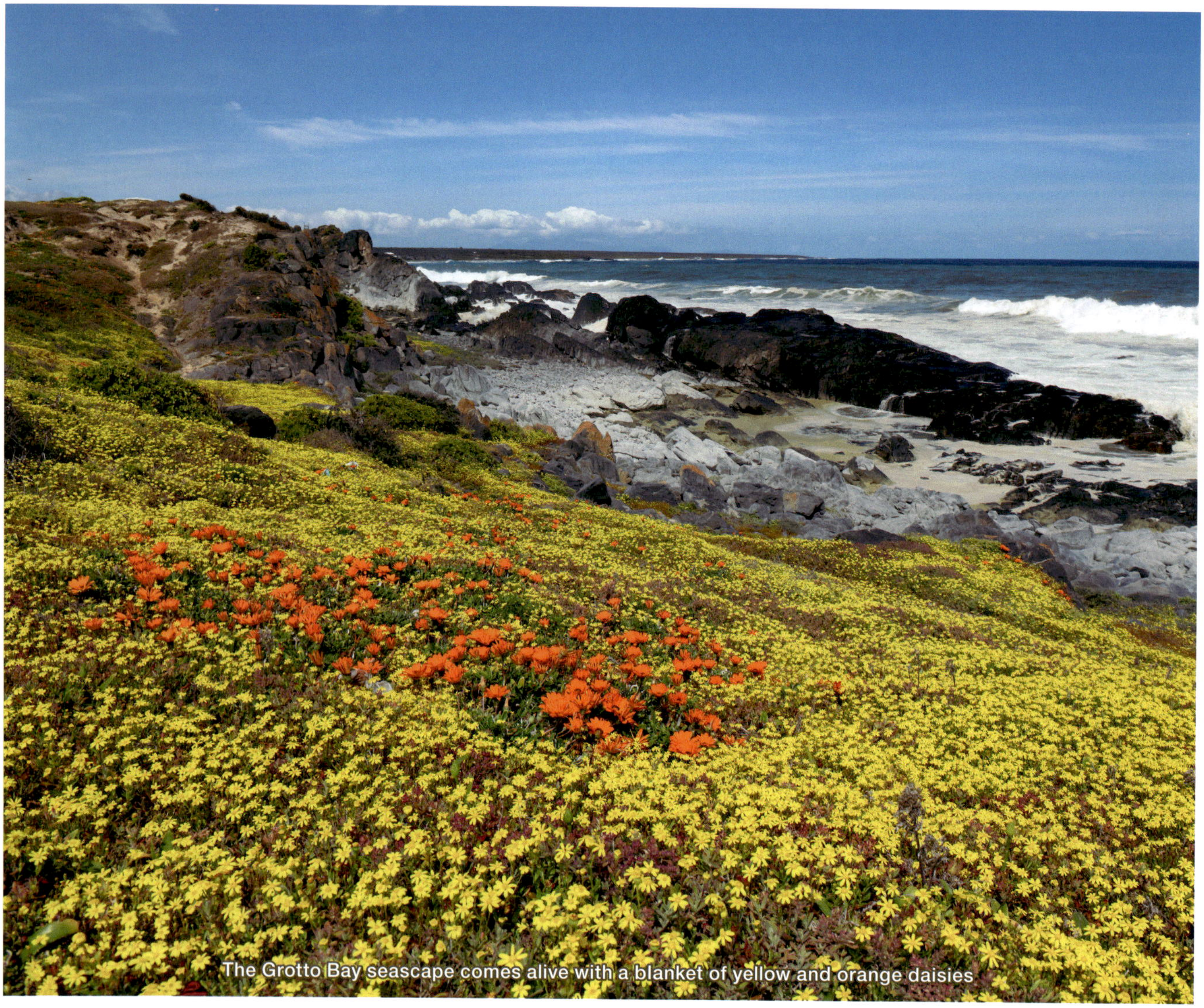

The Grotto Bay seascape comes alive with a blanket of yellow and orange daisies

Grotto Bay

- **Few flower displays from September to October**
- **Coastal fynbos species, dune fynbos, annuals (smaller quantities)**
- **Coastal walks, birding, photography**

The Grotto Bay Coastal and Nature Reserve is a phase of the Cape West Coast Biosphere Reserve, which was designated by UNESCO in 2000. The reserve's primary focus is to ensure ecological sustainability and landscape preservation. The Grotto Bay Coastal Reserve was established in 2002.

The magnificence is incomparable. The coastal area is rugged and untamed, with breathtaking windswept vistas. The primarily untouched village is even more charming, where contemporary and spacious homes grace the dunes, commanding views of the deserted beach. The name 'Grotto' signifies a small cave or cavern, suggesting the bay takes its name from the sea cave on the shoreline.

Hopefield

September

Renosterveld and Sandveld fynbos species, Cape flax, buchu, various bulbs, chincherinchee, viooltjie, white rain daisies

Fynbos show (seasonal), agricultural museum, flower viewing (seasonal), hiking, birding

Founded in 1844 on a farm called Langekuil, the town was initially known as Zoute River owing to the small river flowing through the village. In 1853, it was renamed Hopefield in honour of two Cape Colony government officials who laid out the village: Major William Hope and Auditor General Mr Field.

Originally founded as a Dutch Reformed Church parish, Hopefield grew around the church. The town, situated in a semi-arid agricultural region, primarily produces wheat, but sheep farming and honey production also play significant roles. In the past, Hopefield had a railway connection with Cape Town.

White rain daisies at the base of the towering windmills at the Hopefield wind farm

The banks of the Zoute River at Hopefield are covered in yellow hongerblomme, surings, knopiesopslag and white and yellow daisies

Darling

- Spectacular wildflowers mid to late September to October
- Renosterveld and Sandveld fynbos species, arum lilies, Cape flax, chincherinchee, various bulbs (e.g. *Lachenalia*, *Sparaxis*)
- Evita se Perron, Darling Brew, Groote Post vineyards, Ormonde winery, Darling Sweet, museum, wildflower displays (seasonal), Rocklands bouldering

Wildflower reserves and farms around Darling

Dubbed the 'flower village', Darling is nestled in the heart of a prosperous agricultural region that flourishes for its dairy products, wool, peas, grapes and chincherinchees. Although numerous farms had already been established in the area, Darling was planned and developed in 1853 and emerged around the Dutch Reformed congregation. The local museum chronicles the evolution and lifestyle of the village since its inception.

Darling exudes a rich tapestry of art, tradition and culture. Pieter-Dirk Uys, a prominent South African performer and satirist, thrust Darling into the national spotlight when he acquired the station building and established Evita se Perron.

Despite its intriguing and somewhat deceptive name, Darling originates from Sir Charles Henry Darling, a British lieutenant governor in the mid-1800s. Little did he know the curiosity and fascination the town's identity would spark.

While the landscape is predominantly adorned with a handful of perennial shrubs throughout most of the year, the arrival of spring transforms Darling into a breathtaking spectacle. Over 1 200 species of flowering vegetation burst into a kaleidoscope of colours during this season. Renowned for its wildflowers, Darling has enchanted visitors since 1917 with the annual Darling Wildflower Show, expertly coordinated by the Darling Wildflower Society.

Purple and red kelkiewyn

Geissorhiza eurystigma, known as 'kelkiewyn', is a bulbous perennial endemic to South Africa. Its showy, purple flowers with a distinctive red centre and white ring are a striking sight in the late spring. This geophyte is well adapted to dry conditions, relying on its bulb for nutrient and water storage during dormancy.

Geissorhiza eurystigma

Moraea sp. of the Iris family

Arum lilies, Darling

Chincherinchee, Tienie Versfeld Wildflower Reserve

Nemesia sp. of the *Nemesia* family, Renosterveld Reserve, Darling

Bright pink froetang (*Romulea hirsuta*)
Renosterveld Reserve, Darling

Monsonia speciosa, Tienie Versfeld Wildflower Reserve

Tienie Versfeld Wildflower Reserve

September to October

Sandveld fynbos species, arum lily, chincherinchee, various bulbs, gladiolus

Photography, birding, fynbos walks

In 1958, Marthinus Versfeld generously donated a 22 hectare portion of his farmland to the National Botanical Gardens of South Africa, establishing the Tienie Versfeld Reserve as a dedicated flower reserve. This remarkable sanctuary has never been subjected to ploughing and has been only sporadically grazed by cattle, creating an ideal haven for biodiversity.

The reserve is renowned for its exceptional collection of flowering bulbs and other rare plant species, which owe their splendour to the convergence of diverse veld types: Sandveld, Strandveld, Renosterveld and Rietveld. This unique combination gives rise to a breathtaking variety of flowering bulbous plants and rare species, creating an array of sizes and colours.

Renosterveld, one of the most endangered vegetation types in the world, features fertile soil. Tragically, a significant portion of Renosterveld has been lost to agriculture, primarily as a consequence of wheat farming. Only 2% of the Cape Floristic Region's Renosterveld vegetation types are officially protected, highlighting the urgent need for conservation efforts.

A field of blue flowers (not indigenous) brightens the landscape across from Tienie Versfeld Wildflower Reserve

Tienie Versfeld Wildflower Reserve is abloom with white, scented chincherinchees

Yzerfontein

- **September to October**
- **Coastal fynbos species, dune fynbos, Strandveld species, rooi malva, bietou, viooltjie, some annuals**
- **Eighteen Mile Beach, fishing, whale watching (seasonal), kite surfing, hiking (Dassen Island trail, Bokbaaivygie hiking trail and Scaap island trail)**

Yzerfontein, a charming harbour town on South Africa's west coast, boasts a rich history beyond its 18th century Dutch settlement. Archaeological digs have revealed remnants of food and tools, whispering secrets of the ancient people who called this place home long ago.

The town's name, 'Iron Fountain', sparks debate. Theories range from iron traces in the water to its refreshing coolness or even a dedication to Jurijan Eijser, who investigated the sinking of the Schoonenberg in 1722 in the area.

While its official development began in 1937 by Abraham Katz, Yzerfontein's roots trace back to 1732 when Cornelius Heufke grazed livestock on the farm Eizerfontein. Over time, ownership changed hands, with Nicolas Pienaar selling portions in 1937, paving the way for the Yzerfontein Seaside Estate.

Its true gem remains 16-mile Beach, the longest uninterrupted stretch of sand on South Africa's coastline. This pristine beach borders the West Coast National Park, offering a stunning backdrop for visitors to explore Yzerfontein's unique blend of historical charm and natural beauty.

Red mallow/rooi malva (*Pelargonium fulgidum*)

Vibrant yellow daisies, Yzerfontein

Yellow hongerblomme, Yzerfontein

Rain daisies and hongerblomme intermingle alongside rain pools, Yzerfontein

White and yellow daisies, Postberg Flower Reserve

West Coast National Park and Postberg

✱✱✱✱✱

- Mid to late September to October (Postberg, seasonal)
- Namaqualand daisies, gousblom, gazania, vygies, sporries, chincherinchee, bloubekkie, various bulbs and fynbos species
- Game viewing (eland, zebra, bontebok), birding (especially at Abrahamskraal), hiking (Bonawe Trail), lagoon activities (swimming, kayaking), cycling, picnicking, Kraalbosdam hide

In the past, the area encompassing Oude Post, Nieuwland and Kreeftebaai primarily consisted of farmlands. However, agricultural practices ceased in 1966 when the land was stocked with various wildlife species and, in 1969, the West Coast National Park was officially designated as a nature reserve to safeguard the critical conservation areas of the Langebaan Lagoon, associated wetlands and the offshore islands in Saldanha Bay.

Postberg Flower Reserve, located within the West Coast National Park, is a virtually untouched floral landscape bordering the turquoise waters of Langebaan Lagoon. It enhances the coastal scenery, adorned with sparkling white beaches. Postberg is open to the public during the spring months of August and September, when it transforms into a collage of colourful wildflowers. The hillsides come alive with sweeps of yellow, orange, purple, pink, red and white, creating a captivating sight. The reserve remains closed for the rest of the year to allow for natural regeneration.

No walking in the flower fields, Postberg Flower Reserve

Hongerblomme stretch towards the beach, Plankiesbaai, Postberg Flower Reserve

White, yellow and orange daisies unite to create a masterpiece of colour, Postberg Flower Reserve

Seeberg

- **Mid to late September to October**
- **Coastal fynbos species, dune fynbos, some annuals**
- **Lagoon views, birding, photography, walks**

Perched atop granite boulders overlooking Langebaan Lagoon, Seeberg's tiny historical stone cottage offers breathtaking Postberg vistas. Its construction date by local Dutchman Bollie Penz or Wit Bollie is unknown. The building materials used to build the cabin were sourced from the surrounding area before being carried up in bags.

Penz, who had access to an underground water supply, cultivated a vegetable and fruit garden on the north side of the hill. Some of the trees he planted, such as quince, fig and prickly pear, still thrive today. Penz was a tanner and crafted saddles, ropes and cart tools on the nearby Soutekuilen farm.

In the 1980s, the proprietor of the neighbouring farm, Mooimaak, renovated Bollie's house. Subsequently, the house underwent further improvements and was transformed into an information centre exhibiting a collection of photographs highlighting the park and its surroundings.

Sandveld stinkweed (*Oncosiphon suffruticosus*) flanks the approach to Seeberg House.

Blou sysie (*Geissorhiza aspera*), Seeberg

Kukumakranka, Langebaan

Kukumakranka (*Koekemakranka*)

With the arrival of summer, *Gethyllis*, a threatened genus of *Amaryllidaceae* genus endemic to arid southern Africa, unveils its captivating beauty.

These leafless bulbs reveal fragrant, delicate, short-lived, white-mauve flowers. Starkly contrasting with the barren surroundings, this counterintuitive timing allows the plant to conserve vital energy and resources. Focusing on reproduction when pollinators are most active and competition from other flowering plants is minimal, significantly maximises the plant's chances of successful pollination.

The plant's winter transformation sets it apart. Finger-like, club-shaped fruit rises from the earth. Its fragrant strawberry-like pulp conceals countless seeds within its fleshy embrace. Historically, these aromatic berries were harvested and used to scent rooms and linens, filling homes with a delightful fragrance. At no point are multiple stages of growth simultaneously visible. They bloom in midsummer, fruit in autumn, and produce foliage during the winter months, effectively avoiding the stresses of the dry season.

Langebaan

Mid to late September to October

Coastal fynbos species, dune fynbos, vygies, white rain daisy, sporrie, orange daisies, viooltjies and smaller annuals in surrounding areas

4x4 routes, art galleries, birding, hiking, cycling

Coastal lagoons typically arise from freshwater systems that can be connected to the ocean. However, the Langebaan Lagoon distinguishes itself as a saltwater lagoon owing to its formation during prehistoric times, when sea levels underwent significant changes. Consequently, this lagoon is sustained by the inflow of seawater from the Atlantic Ocean.

Founded around 1870, the town's name is believed to have been given by Dutch sailors who sought shelter in the lagoon to repair and clean their vessels. The name translates to 'long track' or 'long course', referring to the long and tranquil stretch of beach in the area. Langebaan's lagoon, with its varying channels, contributes to its exquisite range of turquoise hues.

While retaining its charm, Langebaan has evolved from a sleepy holiday village into a thriving community. Nestled on the West Coast, it boasts charming fishing villages, pristine white beaches that rival the Caribbean, and crystal-clear waters lapping the lagoon's shores. The surrounding landscape is a tapestry of diverse vegetation dominated by the unique Sandveld fynbos. This delicate floral kingdom is carefully protected by the Parks Board, ensuring Langebaan's natural beauty endures for generations to come.

Langebaan's tidal mud flats and wetlands attract numerous local and migratory bird species, making it an internationally acclaimed Ramsar site.

Lady's hand/blouraaptol (*Cyanella hyacinthoides*), Langebaan

Shark Bay at Langebaan Lagoon is complemented by the surrounding blue sporrie and white rain daisies

Vredenburg

- **September**
- **Scattered annuals, some fynbos remnants in undeveloped areas**
- **Angling club (fishing competitions), shopping, local restaurants, gateway to the West Coast**

Originally named Potgietersrus when founded in 1852, Vredenburg is a charming town with strong Dutch influences rooted in farming and rural living. Despite its current name, which means 'town of peace', Vredenburg was not always peaceful. It was initially named Twisfontein or 'dispute fountain' in Afrikaans because of a water rights dispute between the owners of Heuningklip and Witteklip farms, separated by a freshwater spring. As the parties sought a resolution, the name was changed to Prosesfontein, 'process fountain'. When the dispute was finally resolved, and peace was restored, the name Vredenburg was chosen.

Nowadays, Vredenburg serves as the commercial and transportation hub of the Cape West Coast.

Hongerblomme (*Senecio* sp.) and yellow daisies trace the edges of Vredenburg

Lit up by yellow hongerblomme (*Senecio* sp.), a young swallow begs for food at Vredenburg

Yellow hongerblomme surround the Saldanha steel plant

Saldanha Bay

- Mid to late September to October
- Coastal fynbos species, dune fynbos, smaller annuals
- Harbour tours, Naval Base museum, fishing, birding, whale watching (seasonal), Marcus Island (bird sanctuary)

Saldanha Bay, named initially after Admiral António de Saldanha, who anchored his fleet in the area in 1503, holds an intriguing history. Although De Saldanha never set foot in Saldanha Bay, a Dutch cartographer sailing past Saldanha Bay mistakenly attributed its discovery to him and named it in his honour. However, De Saldanha's valid claim to fame lies in the discovery of Table Bay.

Today, Saldanha Bay has a naval training base and the South African Military Academy. The bay encompasses a pristine nature reserve that transforms into an enchanting floral wonderland during spring. Visitors can enjoy well-established hiking trails and magnificent vantage points to observe the majestic southern right whale during calving season.

The steel industry played a significant role in the regional and national economies in the past. However, the Saldanha Steel plant ceased operations in early 2020 as a result of financial challenges. While some residents considered the steelworks an eyesore and a source of pollution, it employed many individuals. Despite efforts by the Trade and Industry minister to preserve jobs, the closure was inevitable.

Purple suring

Bokbaaivygies, Jacobsbaai

Jacobsbaai

- Mid to late September to October
- Coastal fynbos species, dune fynbos, Namaqualand daisies, gousblom, vygies
- Walks, fishing, photography, birding, wildflower displays (seasonal), quiet

Founded on farmland and later registered as 109 Jacobsbaai, the town is believed to have derived its name from the French trader Jacques Titus. Ships would deploy to the bay to load grain and produce while anchored in its sheltered waters. During the 1800s, the area served as a quarantine location for ships' sick passengers before they arrived in Cape Town.

The picturesque and distinctive area of Jacobsbaai features a rugged coastline with seven charming sandy bays nestled between rocky outcrops. This isolated seafront stretches over 2 km and has breathtaking wildflower displays during spring, earning the region the nickname of 'Namaqualand by the sea'.

White daisies, Jacobsbaai

Blue felicia daisies

Field of poppies (not indigenous) growing outside Jacobsbaai

Paternoster

Mid September to October

Coastal fynbos species, dune fynbos, vygies, rain daisies, smaller annuals

Beach walks, Cape Columbine lighthouse, kayaking, whale watching, fishing, crayfishing (seasonal, permits needed), culinary experiences (renowned restaurants)

Established in 1863, Paternoster is a quaint fishing village along the Atlantic coast that encapsulates the essence of the West Coast, representing its rich history and unique charm. As the oldest fishing village along this coastline, it exudes a blend of contrasts and seasonal beauty. In spring, the landscape becomes adorned with dancing daisies, waving green carpets of wheat in winter, which become dusty in the summer heat.

Paternoster harmoniously fuses timeless beauty with modern comforts. Its unique architectural style stands out, as most of the town's buildings are constructed from locally abundant limestone, giving them a distinctive white-washed appearance.

The town's name has two possible origins. The first suggests it was derived from a type of fishing tackle originating in this place. The second explanation is equally intriguing, as It relates to shipwrecked sailors, who were grateful for their safe arrival on shore, giving the name Paternoster, meaning 'Our Father'.

Before the arrival of European settlers in the early 1800s, the area of Paternoster had been inhabited by San hunter-gatherers for thousands of years. Numerous shell middens in Paternoster are evidence of the early settlement of indigenous hunter-gatherer-fisher communities that thrived by relying on abundant marine resources, such as shellfish, crayfish, seals and marine birds. Archaeological excavations carried out in Paternoster reveal the majority of these shell middens dates back to within the last 3 000–4 000 years, encompassing both the period before and after the arrival of Khoikhoi pastoralists who introduced sheep and pottery to the area.

Paternoster's allure extends beyond its fishing industry. With colourful fishing boats dotting the shore, long stretches of white sandy beaches and rugged fynbos landscapes, the village attracts artists and city dwellers seeking a peaceful and serene environment.

One notable aspect of Paternoster's history involves Johan Carosini, a charismatic hotel operator known for his entertaining stories. In 1974, Carosini began collecting honeymoon panties in the hotel bar, creating the Panty Bar. Although the extensive collection was taken down in 1983 because of legal concerns, Giorello Carosini revived the tradition in the 1990s. Regular donations ensure the Panty Bar continues to entertain international visitors.

Elansvye or suurvye (*Carpobrotus quadrifidus*)

White daisy (*Arctotus* sp.) growing in crayfish exoskeletons

Cape Columbine Nature Reserve and Tietiesbaai

- **Mid to late September to October**
- **Coastal fynbos species, dune fynbos, daisies, vygies**
- **Lighthouse tours, hiking, fishing, camping, photography, wildflower displays (seasonal), coastal scenery**

The Cape Columbine Nature Reserve encompasses a wild and unspoilt area, except for the impressive Columbine lighthouse atop Castle Rock. This manually operated lighthouse, named after a British shipwreck in 1829, serves as a vital warning beacon for passing ships, alerting them to the treacherous dangers along the rugged West Coast. It is often the first lighthouse noticed by sailors approaching Africa.

Covering 263 hectares of rocky shoreline, this pristine coastal reserve is adorned with tranquil bays and coves, including the well-known Tietiesbaai. Proclaiming it a nature reserve in 1973, Cape Nature emphasised the significance of preserving the natural vegetation in this conservation area to safeguard its critical biodiversity.

The origin of the name Tietiesbaai holds intriguing possibilities. One interpretation suggests it may have been inspired by the picturesque hillock, with curves reminiscent of a pair of breasts and a distinctive 'nipple' standing against the scenic skyline. Another plausible explanation for the name is linked to a local French trader, Jacques Titius, or perhaps a fisherman or captain with a similar name, who met a tragic fate in those waters. Interestingly, Pieter Pieterse, a resident of the area, first referred to it as Tietiesbaai, and the name has stuck ever since.

White rain daisies (*Dimorphotheca pluvialis*)

Yellow and white daisies thriving on the coastline's edge

Cape Columbine lighthouse perches atop Castle Rock at the Cape Columbine Nature Reserve

Bright pink vygies, Tietiesbaai

Purple Hermannia (*Hermannia trifurca*)

St Helena Bay

September to October

Coastal fynbos species, smaller annuals

Whale watching (seasonal), dolphin watching, fishing, birding, sheltered bays, Port of St Helena Bay

St Helena Bay, known initially as Bahia de Santa Helena, holds an important place in history owing to its connection with Portuguese explorer Vasco da Gama. In 1497, Da Gama arrived in the bay while searching for a sea route to Asia. The bay was named after Saint Helena, a revered figure, the mother of Constantine the Great.

Nourished by the nutrient-rich Benguela current, the waters of St Helena Bay are abundant with marine life, sustaining the livelihoods of coastal communities. Fish are often sold directly from fishing boats, and the bay is renowned as a prime fishing centre, housing several fish-processing factories. Immerse yourself in the local culture by engaging with the lively and humorous vernacular of the fish-selling women in the harbour.

Known as the 'Bay of bays', St Helena Bay boasts 18 nearby bays. Its strategic location shields it from the strong winds commonly experienced along the West Coast. Interestingly, it is the only place on the West Coast where one can witness the sunrise over the ocean.

Sandy Point serves as the primary harbour in the area, and St Helena Bay is a pivotal point along the Cape Birding Route and the southernmost point of the migratory route from northern Europe. Whales and dolphins frequent the bay for food, with southern right whales particularly prominent during the latter half of the year when they mate and give birth in the sheltered tranquil waters.

Viooltjie (*Lachenalia*)

The banks of Port Owen marina are adorned with *Senecio* daisies, locally known as hongerblomme

Port Owen

- **September**
- **Riverine annuals, some coastal species**
- **Marina activities, river cruises (Berg River), fishing, birding**

Situated between Velddrif and Laaiplek, Port Owen is a picturesque port featuring a delightful marina and yacht club. The port is named after H Owen Wiggins Junior, visionary developer of the marina and its residential plots. Over 15 years, substantial amounts of sand and rock were dredged to construct a 7 km riverside embankment adorned with numerous jetties and a bustling business centre.

The Berg River gracefully curves around three sides of Port Owen, forming 3.5 km of canals and scenic private waterways for serene kayaking. It allows boats to access the river and the sea, making it an ideal location for yachtsmen seeking a safe haven.

St Helena Bay's proximity further enhances Port Owen's appeal as a prime anchorage. This bay, the largest on Africa's West Coast, offers exceptional sailing conditions along the South African shoreline thanks to its sheltered nature and strategic alignment with the prevailing summer winds.

Velddrif and Laaiplek

Mid to late September to October

Riverine annuals, saltmarsh species, rain daisies, lazy daisies, coastal fynbos

Berg River estuary (birding, boat trips), Bokkom Laan (dried fish industry), Velddrif salt pans, fishing, Port Owen marina, Rocherpan Nature Reserve (birding)

Velddrif, a town steeped in history and tradition, appears almost frozen in time. Its origins can be traced to Theunis Smit, a farmer who led his livestock through a natural drift in the veld to find grazing on the other side of the Berg River. The animals would often swim across the river, leading to the construction of a ferry in 1899. This ferry, a significant part of Velddrif's history, became the sole means of crossing the Berg River.

Historically, Velddrif and Laaiplek developed separately based on their geographical locations and trading activities. Laaiplek, located on the western side of the town, closest to the sea, translates to 'loading place'; it thrives on the banks of the Berg River. The pier buzzes with activity, especially in the late afternoons when fishing boats return, unloading their bounty to be weighed and collected by waiting buyers.

The sea and its abundant resources played a pivotal role in attracting settlers to the region, and the development of the community revolved primarily around this natural asset. In the past, the farmers transported the Sandveld's wheat harvest down the Berg River to a storage location near the river mouth at Laaiplek. Smaller boats transported the wheat across the sandbanks, where it awaited larger ships on their journey to Cape Town. In 1968, a channel was created through blasting, connecting the river to St Helena Bay and leading to the construction of Laaiplek's fishing harbour. The historic harbour was once the heart of the local fishing industry. Remnants of fish canneries and processing plants still stand as testaments to its past.

Laaiplek, originally a humble fishing village, has blossomed beyond its fishing roots. Over time, it has practically merged with the neighbouring town of Velddrif, just 2 km inland. Laaiplek's shops and restaurants, nestled near the charming Laaiplek Hotel, seamlessly blend into the larger town.

Velddrif, with its dry summers, provides the perfect environment for extracting salt from seawater, which is why some of South Africa's prominent salt brands chose to establish a factory there.

Framed by the riverbank, Bokkom Laan is a quaint dusty road adorned with a cluster of historic structures and jetties. It derives its name from traditionally preserved salted mullet, known as bokkoms, strung up and dried like biltong. This local delicacy has become a signature of the area.

It charms visitors as a picturesque fishing village where one can immerse oneself in the daily lives of fishermen, explore the river, admire the weathered yet enchanting jetties and colourful wooden boats, and enjoy exceptional birding opportunities.

Lazy daisies (*Foveolina tenella* Asteraceae) in full bloom, Velddrif shooting range

Senecio daisies, or hongerblomme, thrive on the Berg River riverbank at Velddrif

Bokkoms on the line to dry

Field of poppies (not indigenous), outside Velddrif

Dwarskersbos

✱✱

◔ **September to October**

✱ **Coastal fynbos species, dune fynbos, smaller annuals**

⚑ **Beach walks, fishing, swimming, stargazing**

Once a farm belonging to the Smit family, it derived its name from the indigenous wild camphor tree found in the area. It is believed to have provided shelter to travellers in the past. The word Dwarskersbos refers to the practice of setting up camp and positioning ox wagons 'across' or 'transverse' to the wild camphor tree, using its bushes to shelter against prevailing winds. As time passed, a residential community gradually transformed into a serene and peaceful seaside fishing village.

Fishermen cast their lines along this pristine white-sand beach, hoping for a bountiful catch. Anglers can add various species like galjoen, grey mullet, snoek, steenbras, bronze bream, elf (shad), cob, eagle ray, gurnard and white stumpnose to their repertoire.

The lazy daisy is also known as kleinkruid (*Foveolina tenella, Asteraceae*)

Fiery red blooms of the rooibobbejaantjie or strandlelie (*Babiana hirsuta*)

Wamakersvlei

September to October

Sandveld fynbos species, annuals, Livingstone daisy, Bokbaaivygie

Nature walks, birding, farm stays, quiet

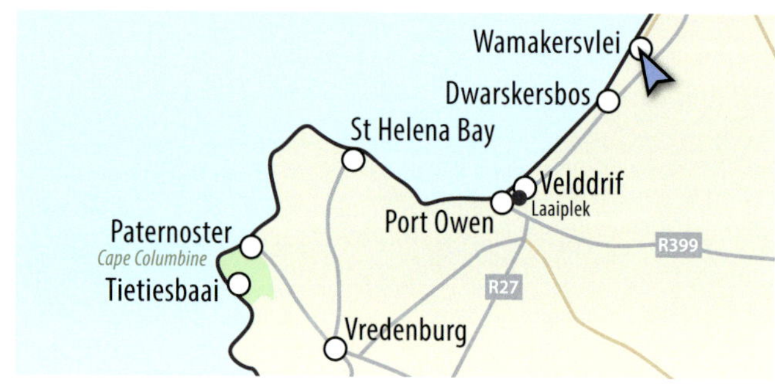

The name translates to 'wagonmakers' wetland', which posed a significant challenge for farmers transporting their crops through the deep sandy soil to Velddrif, where they could be shipped to Cape Town. The sandy road and pans at Wamakersvlei made the journey tough for heavily laden ox wagons, leading farmers to unharness their oxen and repair their wagons at this location.

Wamakersvlei sits next to a chain of salt pans. These pans stretch for 20 km, creating a natural path that simplifies the final leg of transporting goods to the waiting sailboats in Laaiplek, located where the Berg River meets the ocean. Over time, Wamakersvlei became home to the 'viewers', caretakers of the cattle and goats of wealthier farmers. The farm still boasts a pristine 400 hectare wilderness area along a 7 km coastline that borders the Rocher pans.

Today, the historic Fisherman's Village in Wamakersvlei has seen the restoration of the original herdsman cottages. Visitors can reconnect with nature, breathe in the ocean air and fynbos scents, and enjoy the unspoilt 400 hectares of wilderness while following the tracks and trails of indigenous wildlife. The area offers incredible starry nights, radiant sunsets and a scenic 7 km private beach, where one might even encounter cattle grazing along the shore.

Bokbaaivygies (*Cleretum bellidiforme*)

Bokbaaivygies decorate the edge of a pan at Wamakersvlei

Bokbaaivygies (*Cleretum bellidiforme*)

Aurora

Aurora

✻✻

September to October

Renosterveld and Sandveld fynbos species, various annuals

Scenic drives, small town charm, stargazing

It is an enchanting town with captivating vistas. Aurora, a name that whispers of dawn's first light, rests peacefully amid the vastness of the Sandveld.

Established as a spiritual haven for the scattered inhabitants of the region, Aurora embarked on a path of independence in 1906, severing its ties with the Piketberg congregation. In 1866, building work began on a modest church on the farm Rietvlei. The present church, designed by architect WH Ford, rose to completion in 1908. Its first minister was Reverend CR Ferreira, a former Boer prisoner of war in what was then Ceylon (now Sri Lanka). The mark of his homeland remained etched in his heart, for when his daughter received baptism within these very walls, he bestowed upon her the name Ceylonia Aurora, a beautiful echo of both his own heritage and the town's luminous spirit.

Beyond the tranquil village lies McClear Base, a place of pivotal importance. It serves as the northernmost point for all survey beacons in South Africa. In 1751, the esteemed French astronomer Abbé de la Caille began a remarkable journey to unravel the mysteries of the Earth's shape in the southern hemisphere. Armed with the tools of trigonometry, he embarked on a meticulous process. To achieve his goal, De la Caille undertook the incredible feat of walking the distance between this spot and Cape Town a staggering three times! On the farm Klipfontein, just outside the town's embrace, he erected the northernmost beacon. The western beacon found its home on Kasteelberg, while the southernmost one stands sentinel on the corner of Strand and Adderley streets in Cape Town, forever linked to its northern counterpart in Aurora.

The people of Aurora possess a distinctive character. They embody a simple way of life that attracts visitors seeking respite from the turmoil of urban existence. It is not uncommon for individuals to retire or seek solace in this tiny gem in the Sandveld.

Yellow daisies, Cape marigold (*Arctotheca calendula*) and pink and yellow hongerblomme, Aurora

Sheep foraging on a carpet of *Senecio* hongerblomme and other yellow daisies

Tortoise berry (*Muraltia spinosa*)

Redelinghuys in the Sandveld

- **Mid to late September to October**
- **Sandveld fynbos species, various annuals and geophytes**
- **Hiking trails, mountain biking, birding**

Dominated by a church on its main street and nestled amid rocky hills and patches of blue gum trees, Redelinghuys is renowned as the potato capital of the Sandveld. Numerous farms in the Verlorenvlei region produce high-quality potatoes. The town's predominantly Victorian architecture adds to its unique charm and character.

Originally a part of the Wittedrift farm, Sir George Napier bestowed this land in 1841 upon Hendrik Coetzee, who eventually sold it to JNL Redelinghuys. The village derives its name from the latter, who generously donated the land to the Dutch Reformed Church as a token of his unwavering faith.

The Sandveld is a pristine wilderness untouched by human influence. Vast stretches of this land provide a haven for a remarkable diversity of life. From plants and birds to animals, reptiles and insects, all flourish within this unique ecosystem. But the crown jewel of the Sandveld is undoubtedly the explosion of wildflowers that blankets the landscape each spring. This vibrant spectacle is a testament to the region's unparalleled natural beauty and rich biodiversity.

Tortoise berry (*Muraltia spinosa*)

White rain daisies, Klein Tafelberg

Klein Tafelberg

- **Mid to late September to October**
- **Mountain fynbos species, ericas, proteas, restios**
- **4x4 trails, hiking, camping, scenic views**

Situated approximately 23 km north of Aurora, this isolated hill, or inselberg, rises abruptly from a virtually level plain, culminating in an abrupt flat tabletop feature reminiscent of its famous counterpart, Table Mountain, in Cape Town.

Klein Tafelberg catches the eye from all directions but its name can be misleading. The table-like crown is an optical illusion. As one approaches, it becomes evident that what initially appeared to be a flat mountain top is a series of jagged cliffs ascending towards the sky, interspersed with gentle gradients.

The hill is adorned with indigenous fynbos, while the surrounding veld has largely been replaced or is being replaced by wheat fields and cultivated crops.

Verlorenvlei

***

Mid to late September to October

Wetland and riverine species, some coastal and fynbos species in surrounding areas

Wetland, fishing, canoeing, photography, botany

Dating back to 1724, it evokes a sense of serenity regardless of the direction from which it is approached. This unique location conceals fresh water within its reeds, leading to speculation that its name, which means 'lost vlei', stems from early humans wanting to keep this natural wonder a secret to themselves.

Situated in the Western Cape, Verlorenvlei is one of the most vital estuarine systems and extensive natural wetlands along the west coast of South Africa. It is a RAMSAR-protected site. This coastal freshwater lake offers a remarkable array of bird species, making it a haven for avian diversity. Flowing down to Elands Bay, approximately 32 km from Redelinghuys, Verlorenvlei follows its course through breathtaking landscapes.

However, the delicate balance of Verlorenvlei faces challenges, as excessive water extraction by farmers leads to a shallowing of the channel, hindering water flow. During heavy rains, the lake overflows into the sea at the mouth at Elands Bay. Unfortunately, the exchange with the sea is limited, resulting in stagnant and highly saline water forming pools. In the dry summer, water evaporates, causing the collections to dry up entirely or become extremely shallow.

Verlorenvlei

Over time, water sampling has revealed farmers who pump water from the bottom of the vlei irrigate their land with saline water, further exacerbating the situation. Two causeways connect the lake to the sea. Rocks and sand obstruct the natural flow, creating a virtually closed system. The increasing salt concentration persists owing to insufficient rainfall to flush it out. Some farmers hastily block the causeways to retain as much water as possible for irrigation. Fluctuating water levels throughout the year greatly impact the distribution of plants and animals vital to the wetland's ecosystem.

White rain daisies close to Vensterklip

Eland's Bay

✳✳

- **September to October**
- **Coastal fynbos species, dune fynbos, some annuals, pietsnot, rain daisies, lazy daisies**
- **Surfing (famous left-hand break), birding (Baboon Point), rock art (San paintings), fishing, beach walks**

A coastal town with a rich history dating back over 80 000 years to the Middle Stone Age. The mountain that skirts the bay where the town stands descends towards the sea at Baboon Point, near where a magnificent cave was intermittently inhabited during the Later Stone Age until about 500 years ago, when dwindling food resources and increasing aridity along the coast led the last residents of Eland's Bay cave to abandon the shelter. Though difficult to accurately date, the rock art paintings at Baboon Point provide evidence of the San people who once roamed the region.

Remarkable paintings of large eland, smaller antelope and other animals adorn the cave walls. These ancient artworks feature numerous tiny handprints, some of which are believed to be those of children and young teenagers, overlaying older paintings intertwined with a few human figures. Although eland no longer inhabit the area, it is believed the present day town derived its name from these magnificent grazing creatures. Despite their absence, the name Eland's Bay persistently illustrates the town's enduring cultural and natural heritage.

Initially a crayfish town, Eland's Bay witnessed the emergence of the crayfish industry on the West Coast around the 1890s. While evading rapid development, it managed to preserve its charm. For surfers, Eland's Bay holds sacred status as a coastline. Renowned as the Left Break, the area boasts expansive and consistent waves, drawing surfers to its shores.

Additionally, from July to December, the bay transforms into a prime location for observing migrating southern right whales, Heaviside's dolphins and the occasional appearance of orcas (killer whales). Eland's Bay, a hidden gem, seamlessly blends natural beauty, cultural significance and recreational opportunities for all to enjoy.

Vibrant blooms of Pietsnot (*Grielum humifusum*), Eland's Bay

Leipoldtville

- **Mid to late September**
- **Agricultural annuals, some fynbos remnants**
- **Agricultural scenery, quiet village experience, stargazing**

The town was named after Reverend CF Leipoldt, a Dutch Reformed minister at Clanwilliam from 1884 until 1910, and the father of the more famous CF Louis Leipoldt, born in Worcester in 1880. CF Louis Leipoldt was not only a renowned and prolific South African writer, with works encompassing poetry and cookbooks, but also a compassionate and innovative medical practitioner who dedicated his life to serving patients across the country. During his medical studies in London, CF Louis Leipoldt had the opportunity to train as a cook under the esteemed French chef Auguste Escoffier.

Leipoldtville is beloved for its challenging 4X4 trails, rich history, strong community and pride in its heritage.

White rain daisies or sôe (*Dimorphotheca pluvialis*) beside the ruins at Leipoldtville

Lambert's Bay

- Mid to late September
- Coastal fynbos species, dune fynbos, vygies, some annuals, rain daisies and lazy daisies
- Island Nature Reserve (Cape gannets, seals), Malkoppan cave, crayfishing (seasonal, permits needed), harbour, whale watching (seasonal), dolphin watching

Lambert's Bay owes its name to Lambert von Louvain, a respected German businessman who arrived in the area in the late 19th century. At that time, Von Louvain was responsible for conducting marine surveys and charting maps of the south-west coast of the Cape Colony. One of the inlets he surveyed included a small bay that would later become Lambert's Bay.

In the 1880s, Lambert established a trading station in the area and gained the admiration of the locals for his fair and honest dealings. When the town was officially established in 1922, it was named Lambert's Bay in his honour.

Lambert's Bay has emerged as a sought-after tourist destination renowned for its breathtaking beaches, diverse bird and animal life, and delectable seafood. The town is home to a large colony of Cape gannets and gives visitors an opportunity to observe seals, dolphins and whales in the coastal waters. One of the highlights is the annual Crayfish Festival, eagerly anticipated by both locals and tourists, which celebrates the abundance of this sought-after delicacy.

Vibrant flower fields stretching out near Wadrift

The flower fields opposite Muisbosskerm are alive with a vibrant tapestry of hongerblomme, daisies and vygies

Doringbaai

- **Late August to September**
- **Coastal fynbos species, dune fynbos, some annuals, hongerblomme, rain daisies**
- **Lighthouse, crayfish industry, coastal walks, fishing, wine tasting, quiet harbour atmosphere**

Previously known as Thorn Bay, it is a beautiful fishing village on the West Coast. The exact origin of its name remains vague as it could be attributed to the abundance of thorns in the area or to a description of the adjacent land.

Historically, Doringbaai served as a stopover for ships travelling along the coast. Supplies destined for further transport inland were transferred to the shore using rowing boats and then taken to Vanrhynsdorp with the assistance of camels. Although the original aluminium lighthouse, built in 1963, was destroyed in a violent storm, it has since been replaced by a prominent white lighthouse with a black band and a white lantern house, acting as a guiding beacon for tourists and fishermen.

Adjacent to it stands the original Oceana factory building, which has been transformed into a wine cellar and tasting room called Fryer's Cove. Doringbaai's primary economic activity revolves around the packaging and export of crayfish. While the area's mineral resources may be dwindling, marine diamond mining boats continue to venture out to sea, extracting alluvial diamonds from the seabed. Doringbaai is also frequented by various bird species, including flamingos and pelicans as they approach nearby Eland's Bay.

A golden carpet of *Senecio* hongerblom, offering a view over Doringbaai harbour and the lighthouse

View over the daisies to Strandfontein and the ocean

Strandfontein

- Few displays in late August to September
- Coastal fynbos species, dune fynbos, vygies, Namaqualand daisies
- Beach, fishing, birding, caravan park, sunset views

Strandfontein means 'beach fountain', which is derived from a seaside fountain where the earliest residents, the San and Khoi communities, would quench their thirst with fresh water.

Initially serving as a modest beach resort for Namaqualand farmers, Strandfontein has blossomed into a popular tourist destination, particularly during the flower season. Sandstone outcrops in Strandfontein possess a unique and enchanting presence, and the elevated cliffs make it an ideal vantage point for observing whales during the late winter and early spring months.

Daisies line the edge of a quiet dirt road at Strandfontein

Papendorp

- **Few displays in late August to September**
- **Riverine annuals, salt marsh species and some coastal plants**
- **Small village living, estuary, bird hide**

This charming village along the Olifants River estuary offers picturesque views of the surrounding wetlands. Over time, numerous families were drawn to the area, establishing their homes near the Van Papendorp homestead. By the early 1800s, the region had acquired the name Papendorp, reflecting its growing prominence. As the years passed, Papendorp grew and developed essential amenities. In 1845, it proudly boasted an Anglican Church and a school, solidifying its reputation as a community. By the 1860s, Papendorp had garnered recognition as a residential suburb, attracting those seeking a desirable place to have their home.

Employing traditional processing methods, the inhabitants of Papendorp derive their livelihood from fishing in the estuary with handmade fishing nets and harvesting salt from the nearby salt pans. It is one of the rare places throughout the West Coast that embody the essence of simple living, reminiscent of times long past throughout the West Coast.

A hidden gem, accessible only by foot along a wooden walkway, awaits at the estuary where the river meets the sea. Shimmering saltpans and marshy areas unfold, leading to a bird hide that promises an unforgettable encounter with nature.

Vygies growing on the roof of a Papendorp ruin

Wildflowers adorn the banks of the Olifants River estuary in Papendorp

Vygie

COMMON FLOWER FAMILIES

Daisies

Asteraceae (former Compositeae)

Daisy Family

The defining feature is the capitulum or dense flower head with a dense cluster of many **small flowers** (florets) sitting on a common receptacle, surrounded by bracts, giving the appearance of a single flower.
Disk florets are at the centre and **ray florets** are the strap shaped petal-like florets on the margin.

Typical daisy flower shape

Dimorphotheca sinuata
Namaqualand daisy

Dimorphotheca pinnata
Parachute daisy

Dimorphotheca pluvialis
Rain daisy

Arctotis fastuosa
Bittergousblom

Arctotus sp.
Arctotis gousblom

Gorteria diffusa
Beetle daisy

Cotula sp.
Buttons/Knopiesopslag

Foveolina tenella
Lazy daisy

Senecio cardaminifolius
Geelhongerblom

Felicia sp.
Astertjie/sambreeltjie

Othonno sp.
Bobbejaankool

Succulents

Aizoaceae (Mesembryanthemoidea)

Ice Plant or Mesemb Family (vygies)

The combination of **many petaloid staminodes**, **succulent habit**, and an **inferior ovary** are the most distinctive floral features.

Typical succulent flower

Cleretum bellidiforme
Bokbaaivygie

Apatesia helianthoides
Brakslaai

Drosanthemum sp.
Mauve vygie

Cleretum sp.
Yellow vygie

Monilaria obconica
White vygie

Argyroderma sp.
Stone plant/Bababoudjie

Argyroderma sp.
Stone plant

Carpobrotus quadrifidus
Elandsvye or suurvye

Geophytes

Iridaceae

Iris Family

The flowers have an **inferior ovary**, with a **unique floral symmetry** and **petal styles** (tepals in two whorls, three outer sepals and three inner petals). Plants with a **rhizome**, **corm** or **bulb**.

Moraea sp.
Iris

Moraea miniata
Tulip

Ixia rapunculoides
Bluebells

Geissorhiza aspera
Blousysie

Romulea hirsuta
Froetang

Geissorhiza radians
Kelkiewyn

Babiana hirsuta
Rooibobbejaantjie/strandlelie

Lapeirousia silenoides (Endemic)
Meidestert

Amaryllidaceae

Amaryllis Family

The most important characteristic is that flowers typically have **inferior ovaries** and **umbel-like inflorescences**, often subtended by **a pair of membranous bracts**, **six tepals** and the presence of an **underground bulb**.

Haemanthus amarylloides
Pienkkwas

Brunsvigia bosmaniae
Fragrant candelabra lily

Gethyllis villosa
Kukumakranka

Aspodelaceae

Aloe Family

Flowers often borne in an inflorescence, with a **superior ovary**, **six free tepals** (that are usually free or slightly fused and arranged in two whorls), and a typically **rosette-based** (often succulent) habit.

Aloidendron dichotomum (formerly Aloe dichotoma)
Quiver tree/kokerboom

Trachyandra falcata
Veldkool

Bulbinella sp.
Red katstert

Hyacinthaceae

Hyacinth Family

Bulbous plants, flowers with a **superior ovary** and **six tepals** fused into a **tubular perianth** (fused calyx and corolla).

Ornithogalum thyrsoides
Chincherinchee

Lachenalia sp.
Viooltjie

Colchicum capense ssp. *ciliolatum*
Kokerdoosblom

Other flower families

Brassicaceae

Mustard/Cabbage Family

The **four petals** arranged in a cross, **four sepals** and **four long** and **two short stamens** are the most important floral traits.

Heliophila sp.
Sporrie

Heliophila sp.
White sporrie

Oxalidaceae

Sorrel Family

A flower with **five free petals**, **10 stamens** in two whorls of five (often unequal in length), and leaves that are typically **trifoliate**.

Oxalis sp.
Suring

Malvacease

Hibiscus Family

A central tube of **fused stamens** surrounding the **style** is the most important and diagnostic feature.

Hermannia sp.
Doll's rose

Neuradaceae

Desert Primrose Family

The **inferior, multi-carpellary ovary** with numerous stamens and **spiny dry fruit** are the most important characteristics.

Grielum humifusum
Pietsnot

Scrophulariaceae

Sutera/Figwort Family

Bilateral symmetric flowers, often with a distinct **upper** and **lower lip** formed by five fused petals. **Four stamens** and a **superior ovary**.

Nemesia sp.
Cape jewels

Hemimeris sp.
Bobbejaangesiggies

Manulea sp.
Mauve manulea

Bokhorinkie (*Diascia namaquensis*), Nieuwoudtville

Peachy *Moraea* sp. tulips bloom among an old ruin, on the way to Nieuwoudtville

ABOUT THE AUTHOR

Heléne Venter

Heléne Venter

Born in Cape Town, South Africa, in the late sixties, Heléne spent over 38 years living in the remote Namaqualand region. She developed a profound appreciation for its alluring floral vistas. Despite the seemingly desolate landscape, she was inspired by the beautiful seasonal transformation and captured its enchanting essence through her camera lens.

In 2010, she relocated to Somerset West, expanding her photographic journey to include the West Coast, Nieuwoudtville and the floral landscapes of the Hantam Karoo. With a diverse career spanning several decades in fashion design and photography, Heléne has a fine artistic eye and is motivated by a love of travel and exploration.

Her work is infused with a haunting, evocative quality that invites viewers into a natural and beautifully moving world. In addition to landscapes, her portfolio includes underwater, aerial, studio, portrait, fine art, macro and fashion photography.

Her devotion to her craft has created a unique expression of vibrant artistry that celebrates the hidden richness and beauty waiting to be discovered in even the most unexpected places.

A lone windpump watches over the orange daisies at Namaqua National Park

REFERENCES

Bregman, J (2010). Land and Society in the Komaggas region of Namaqualand. University of Cape Town.

Cairncross, Bruce (2004). History of the Okiep copper district: Namaqualand, Northern Cape Province, South Africa.

Fleminger, David (2020). More than Daisies. Dogdog Publishing.

Nell, Leon (2021). The West Coast: From Melkbos to the Orange River. Penguin Random House. Print Matters Heritage

Raper, PE. Dictionary of Southern African Place Names. Head, Onomastic Research Centre, HSRC.

SAHO South African history online

Schrauwen, Johan, Pickford, Peter (1991). West Coast: A circle of seasons in South Africa. Struik Publishers.

Smalberger, John M (1975). A History of Copper Mining in Namaqualand. Struik Publishers.

The Mineralogical Record (Vol. 35, Issue 4). The Mineralogical, Inc.

Thomas, David G (2011). The Men who would not March: The Surrender of Concordia, Namaqualand, April 1902.

Van Wijk, Calvin S. Rhenish Mission Society in South Africa. 1829–1965.

Note from the author:

My sincere gratitude extends to Jean Smith for her dedicated assistance in editing this book.

www.amanzitrails.co.za

www.ancestors.co.za

www.aridexperiences.com

www.birdlife.org.za

www.boundless-southernafrica.org

www.britannica.com

www.capenamibia.com

www.cradleofhumanculture.co.za

www.experiencenortherncape.com

www.grottobay.org

www.karoo-southafrica.com

www.koingnaas.com

www.mapcarta.com

www.namakwa-info.co.za/region

www.namaqualandflowerfestival.co.za

www.nature-reserve.co.za

www.nieuwoudtville.com

www.paternosterhotel.co.za

www.paternosterproperty.co.za

www.peaceparks.org

www.protectthewestcoast.org

www.pza.sanbi.org

www.route27sa.com

www.saflii.org

www.sahistory.org.za

www.sahris.sahra.org.za

www.sanparks.org

www.sa-venues.com

www.showmesa.co.za

www.southafrica.co.za

www.thefynbosguy.com

www.thegrowcery.co.za

www.thegrowcery.co.za

www.theheritageportal.co.za

www.trailforks.com

www.west-coast-info.co.za

www.westcoastway.co.za

www.westerncape.gov.za

ALPHABETICAL INDEX

MAP INDEX
NORTHERN CAPE
WESTE
Port Nolloth 66
McDougall's Bay
64 Steinkopf
Aggeneys
Pofadder
14
Concordia
56
Nababeep 58
54 Okiep
50 Goegap
44 Springbok
Buffels
Grootmis
69 Kleinzee
67
Naries
68
Komaggas
Wildeperdehoek Pass
77
Shipwreck 4x4 trail
Namaqua National Park (Skilpad)
80
72
Soebatsfontein
Bowesdorp
84
87 Kamassies
86 Rooifontein
70
Koingnaas
78 Kamieskroon
Hondeklipbaai 71
89 Leliefontein
Wallekraal
Spoeg
7
88 Karas
Spoegrivier Mouth
96
Klipfontein
Garies 90
Kliprand
Groen
Groenrivier Mouth
95
Rietpoort
97 Bitterfontein
130 Loeriesfontein
Doring
Nuwerus 100
Sout
128 Quiver Tree Forest
Hantam
Nieuwoudtville Waterfall
Gannabos
Rondekop
125
Knersvlakte
102
Brand se Baai
Landplaas
116 Nieuwoudtville
120 Hantam
Hol
Oorlogskloof
Matjiesfontein
Boereplaas
124
125
Papkuilsfontein
Calvinia
Lutzville
147
Olifants
104 Vanrhynsdorp
106 Maskam
Vredendal 146
132 Klawer
Papendorp 206
Strandfontein 205
Doringbaai 204
Olifants
7
Lambert's Bay 203
Graafwater
134 Clanwilliam
Ramskop
138
139
Biedouw Valley
202 Leipoldtville
Tankwa Karoo
Eland's Bay 200
199
Verlorenvlei
Sandberg
Wupperthal
Cederberg
Rooi Cederberg Karoo Park
Olifants
Redelinghuys
197
198
Klein Tafelberg
142 Citrusdal
Wamakersvlei
Dwarskersbos 194
St Helena Bay
192
196 Aurora
Kagga Kamma
186
188
187 Velddrif
Port Owen
Paternoster 182
Cape Columbine 184
Tietiesbaai
172 Vredenburg
Piketberg
Beaverlac
Jacobsbaai 178
Saldanha Bay 175
Langebaan
157 Hopefield
Koringberg
Porterville
170
168 Seeberg
Grootwinterhoek
166
West Coast National Park
Moorreesburg
Tulbagh
Tienie Versfeld
Yzerfontein 164
162 158 Darling
Riebeek Wes
Riebeek Kasteel
Ceres
Bokkeriviere
Grotto Bay 156
Ganzekraal 154
Mamre
Malmesbury
7
Wellington

Bitterfontein

First edition, first impression 2025
ISBN 978-0-6398580-3-6
Text by Heléne Venter
Photography by Heléne Venter
Publisher: Heinrich van den Berg
Edited and proofread by Margy Gibson
Botanical consultation by Annelise le Roux
Design, typesetting and reproduction by
Heinrich van den Berg and Nicky Wenhold
Printed in China

Published by **HPH Publishing**
50A Sixth Street, Linden, Johannesburg, 2195, South Africa
www.hphpublishing.co.za
info@hphpublishing.co.za

HPH
Publishing

Bitterfontein